Leading and Managing Staff through Challenging Times

Simon Williams

Andrew Macalpine

Colin McCall

London: The Stationery Office

A CIP catalogue record for this book is available from the British Library

First published 2001

ISBN 0 11 702630 1

Printed in the United Kingdom by The Stationery Office Ltd, London
TJ4801 C10 9/01

Published by The Stationery Office and available from:

The Stationery Office
(mail, telephone and fax orders only)
PO Box 29, Norwich NR3 1GN
General enquiries/Telephone orders 0870 600 5522
Fax orders 0870 600 5533

www.thestationeryoffice.com

The Stationery Office Bookshops
123 Kingsway, London WC2B 6PQ
020 7242 6393 Fax 020 7242 6394
68–69 Bull Street, Birmingham B4 6AD
0121-236 9696 Fax 0121 236 9699
33 Wine Street, Bristol BS1 2BQ
0117 926 4306 Fax 0117 929 4515
9–21 Princess Street, Manchester M60 8AS
0161 834 7201 Fax 0161 833 0634
16 Arthur Street, Belfast BT1 4GD
028 9023 8451 Fax 028 9023 5401
The Stationery Office Oriel Bookshop,
18–19 High Street, Cardiff CF1 2BZ
029 2039 5548 Fax 029 2038 4347
71 Lothian Road, Edinburgh EH3 9AZ
0870 606 5566 Fax 0870 606 5588

The Stationery Office's Accredited Agents
(see Yellow Pages)

and through good booksellers

Contents

Contents

List of figures

Professional Excellence in Schools

The Professional Excellence in Schools programme endeavours to deliver authoritative information and professional guidance to education management teams in clear and easily accessible formats.

Professional Excellence in Schools is produced for The Stationery Office by a fully integrated team of expert education professionals and established content providers. We are dedicated to delivering the Professional Excellence in Schools programme to the highest standard. We consider it a key source of information and guidance to facilitate the management of schools and the professional development of the education community.

Each series within Professional Excellence concentrates on a core management function and is designed to provide education professionals with the complete management solution.

Introduction to the series

The purpose of this series of short books is to make available readable,
up-to-date views on educational issues and controversies connected with
school leadership and management. The principal aim is to provide texts
which will support individual and collective professional learning to those
new to school leadership roles, and those aspiring to take on leadership
responsibilities. The series should also help serving headteachers and
governors to review topics of relevance to the implementation of their roles
and responsibilities.

This series attempts to provide general coverage of leadership and
management issues. Its focus is upon motivating and developing people,
thereby sustaining and improving the learning process and schools as a
whole. The titles in this series take a pragmatic approach to understanding
leadership and how it links with corporate decisions and corporate
activities. They also look in more detail at human and systems aspects of
leadership and how these connect with the change process. The general
approach is to try to provide information of wide practical relevance,
supported by problem-solving activities which engage the reader as a
reflective practitioner.

The basic structure is the same across all of the books, thus providing a
uniformity of approach, but the strengths and expertise of each team of
authors is used to the full. The individual authors have been encouraged to
give a personal interpretation of their topic and the way it is developing. To
ensure consistency and relevance, the team responsible for the series has
met on numerous occasions to ensure that the books draw on practical
experience and actual school contexts. By this means, the team has also
sought to minimise the amount of overlap between titles.

The reader is presented with a variety of types of information and this is
used to both stimulate and inform. The common structure in each chapter
in each book includes:

◆ 'Issues in focus' sections. These expand upon the core text by examining
   topical issues of relevance, or they serve to provide further comments on
   a key issue.

◆ Notice board information. Like a school's notice boards, these short sections are there to highlight key messages succinctly or to relay important items of communication.

◆ 'Interesting facts' seek to place key issues in the context of historical, cultural or topical material.

◆ Strategic PIN downs are practical tasks. They are designed to help the reader consider how the content may be taken further, applied to a specific managerial task, or used as a professional development activity by self and/or colleagues.

The overarching aim of the series is to provide short, portable and accessible texts which go some way towards unifying the theory and practice of leadership and management.

Preface

The *School Leadership* series aims to provide a short and concise, but detailed and highly accessible account, of selected areas of leadership theory and practice.

The first book covered leadership in general terms. It examined the concept of leadership and its application by individuals and teams. It emphasised the collective nature of effective practice. This second book builds on that foundation. It looks at the core of any leader's role or leadership group's task – leading and managing staff. It recognises that a lot is asked of people in schools and that the pressures on them as individuals and professional teams is increasing all the time. It traces initial reactions to the government's ambitious goals for education and looks at the continuing call for more radical change. The main content then centres around these two aspects of practice – leading and managing staff in challenging times.

Like the first book, the approach is to blend practical advice with cross-reference to informed opinion and applied research. Much use is made of actual case scenarios to illustrate leadership in practice. The scenarios cover both positive and negative outcomes, since the authors believe in Henry Ford's maxim that 'failure is only the opportunity to begin again more intelligently'.

The book is written from a foundation of leadership practice. Every member of the author team has led well at times, not so well at others. We know from experience that leadership is influenced by inherited circumstances as well as by training and the application of expertise. It often means rising above mere status to steer and inspire. And since it is not a science but a craft, there can be no sure-fire rules or guaranteed strategies. What follows is an attempt to describe the current context in which school leaders find themselves, coupled with descriptions and analyses of different styles of leadership in practice. We have also looked at peak and marginal performance, teamwork and related aspects of professional development.

We hope the book will help new and long-standing leadership teams:

◆ to think through their leadership qualities, style and strategies;
◆ to refresh their thinking and energies;
◆ to continue to lead and manage staff with courage, consistency and effective communication through challenging times.

James Baldwin

'Not everything that is faced can be changed. But nothing can be changed until it is faced.'

School leaders and government reform

Overview

In any country a number of influences shape the education system and the types of schools available. These influences change with political direction and controls, and to a lesser extent with shifts in moral values and social conditions. The freedom of schools and headteachers to choose curriculum, learning outcomes and pedagogy varies with the amount of central and local control they have to contend with at any given point in time. In turn, these controls reflect how far the prevailing climate of national governance is ideological and tightly autocratic, or liberal and democratic. Since these factors influence the degree of central prescription on the curriculum, the manner in which it may be taught and the main techniques used to assess the outcomes, the core of this chapter examines recent centrally initiated reforms and their effects on the principal agents for school change, the teachers. It moves on to consider some aspects of the change process and their implications for school culture and school leadership.

An agenda of reform

'How much easier it is to be critical than to be correct.'

Benjamin Disraeli

The main preoccupation of school leaders since the 1988 Education Reform Act has been to carry out an extraordinarily ambitious government reform programme. This is expected to transform Britain's education system into the best in the world. Towards achieving this goal, the government of the day created a new power structure. This shifted control away from the professionals and towards the consumers and the state with the new arrangement underpinned by business values, some of which were in conflict with those held in the public sector.

School leaders have faced heightened and extensive challenges since 1988: they have had to adjust to new power arrangements, take on new roles, manage innovation at breakneck speed and 'deliver' on results. They have also had to re-examine their own values. Critically, they have been faced with the task of persuading teachers to adjust to the new realities and to give of their best, at a time of rapid change, uncertainty and anxiety.

Current pupil performance indicators show that the profession has responded well to the new agenda. GCSE results have improved steadily and there has been a sharp improvement in Key Stage 2 results. External evaluation of the literacy and numeracy strategies concluded that there had been 'very impressive results in literacy' and 'significant gains in numeracy'. In 1999 a basics skills survey found nearly 20% of 19-year-olds could barely function at work or in society because of their low levels of literacy and numeracy. This chronic problem will probably be virtually eliminated in the future as a result of the literacy and numeracy interventions.

Where the statistics point to continuing underperformance – such as Key Stage 2 handwriting, Key Stage 3 standards, and pupil achievement in schools serving deprived communities – the present government has produced action plans to deal with the problem. Ambitious targets have been set to secure continuing improvement, with additional resources tied in part to local authorities and schools meeting these. The central government drive has generated, according to Tate (1999):

> 'a mood change in schools. There is a new sense that every year they are trying to do better than their previous best . . . they are committed to continuous improvement.'

Teacher morale and job satisfaction

> 'Education helps you earn more. But not many school teachers can prove it.'

Anonymous

Critics of government policy, such as Morley and Rassool (1999), see the position differently:

> 'a central paradox of new managerialism in education is the way in which output has been ostensibly enhanced at the same time as stress, low morale, low recruitment and early retirement amongst educators have increased. The discourse of regulation and blame is driving teachers out of the profession *en masse* and creating a crisis in recruitment.'

p. 61

What does the evidence from surveys, questionnaires and statistical surveys carried out in 2000 show about the condition of the teaching force?

(See NAHT 2000; OECD 2000; School Teachers' Review Body 2000; Stress Teacherline 2000.)

◆ Teachers are working long hours. These are (a) longer than their counterparts in OECD (Organization for Economic Cooperation and Development) countries by an average of 98 hours a year and (b) longer than they worked six years ago by an average of four hours a week. In term time, classroom teachers are working an average of 52 hours a week and headteachers an average of 60 hours a week.

◆ The overload problem is particularly acute in the primary sector where (a) teachers have had to become competent in teaching the National Curriculum in ten different subjects; (b) despite recent improvements, pupil–teacher ratios are higher than on the continent and in UK secondary schools; and (c) teachers have very little or no non-contact time.

◆ Incidents of stress and health problems related to teaching have become much more common. A survey carried out by the counselling service 'Teacherline' in May 2000 concluded that two teachers in five had experienced major stress. One recent survey of workplace stress in Britain concluded that 25% of teachers were now suffering from serious symptoms of stress.

◆ Causes of stress that affect some headteachers and staff are inspections by the Office for Standards in Education (OFSTED) and an overload of work affecting life outside school. Particular causes of stress for some headteachers are dealing with governors and violent parents; for some teachers, causes of stress are dealing with disruptive pupils and bullying headteachers.

◆ Large numbers of heads and teachers have left the profession, either going into alternative employment or taking early retirement. It has been very difficult to fill both vacant headships in primary schools serving deprived areas and teaching posts in a number of subjects in secondary schools.

The way teachers feel about themselves in the context of their work influences whether they stay in teaching and how well they do their job. The evidence referred to above by no means applies to all teachers, nor all schools, as our case studies in Chapter 3 demonstrate. Nevertheless, the overall picture seems to be a gloomy one. It highlights the enormity of the challenge facing school leaders: how to demonstrate a continuing rise in standards in their schools while coping with the pressures upon themselves and extracting the best from their teachers – members of a beleaguered profession characterised, in general, by high levels of stress and low morale (see pp. 122–4). What has brought this situation about?

Change and stress

‘When you take the bull by the horns . . . what happens is a toss up.’

William Pett Ridge

According to Evans (1996):

‘Psychologists and medical researchers have persistently found a connection between change and stress. It is now axiomatic that the greater degree of change one faces . . . the more likely are we to develop physical and psychological symptoms of stress.’

p. 27

Change that is welcomed, for example promotion or a new baby, can increase pressure and this may result in stress. Change that is seen as threatening can cause intense levels of stress particularly when, as in the case of the government reform programme:

◆ it is top–down change imposed from outside;
◆ it conflicts with the dominant value system and culture of the profession;
◆ pressure is seen to outweigh support.

Of course, as was suggested in the first book in this series (McCall and Lawlor 2000), there is no simple definition of stress and no simple menu of response. The word takes on many different meanings in professional development activities and in the research and other literature. The best approach is a preventative one, whereby employers help combat potential stress in the workplace by clarifying roles and responsibilities, giving staff greater control over their own professional affairs, encouraging peer support and, when possible, reducing workloads. Recent research evidence indicates such strategies are more effective than staff attending tailor-made stress-reduction courses (Briner, work in progress, Birkbeck College, University of London).

Top–down change

> 'Everybody is in favour of progress. It's the change they don't like.'   Anonymous

Change is less stressful when those involved have a say in the direction of the change and how it will be made. Government reform was founded on the premise that the views, habits and practices of teachers and, indeed, of the whole educational establishment were at the root of the problem of low standards. Any active consent to the programme was unlikely to be forthcoming, especially as the solution involved attacking teacher autonomy. Hence reform has been driven from the centre with minimum consultation with the profession and its representatives. The programme itself can be seen as having three distinct tracks (see Figure 1).

In the first track, schools were given responsibility for managing their own budgets and, within defined limits, for determining their priorities. In the second track, schools have been made much more accountable for their performance through a national system of assessment, regular inspection and the annual publication of results. In the third track, schools have been given the task of ensuring that pupils become adaptable lifelong learners. Recently there has been more emphasis on the third track with the recognition that this is a critical area if schools are to prepare young people for a post-industrial economy and a post-modern society, characterised by Hargreaves (1994) as a world:

> 'in which problems are unpredictable, solutions are unclear, and demands and expectations are intensifying'.   p. 245

Nevertheless, the second track, with the focus on outcomes, has been and remains the dominant one. Failure to meet the required outcomes results in penal sanctions, principally OFSTED determining whether a school is failing and therefore requiring special measures, and the Department for Education and Skills (DFES) deciding whether to close it down. As the government's special educational adviser has conceded:

> 'The sustained drive from central government is perceived as an entirely top–down reform with its associated pressures to conform, whereas all the evidence suggests that successful reform requires a combination of top–down and bottom–up change.'   Barber 2000

5

Figure 1: The ongoing reform of public education: the three-track analysis

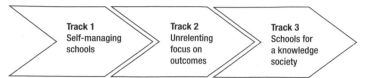

Track	Examples	Vision
1 Self-management	• Locally managed/ grant maintained (UK) • Charter movement (USA) • Schools of the future (Victoria, Australia)	Efficient and effective schools allocating resources to meet their priorities
2 Focus on outcomes	• OFSTED • Target-setting • Literacy/numeracy • League tables • Education Action Zones	High-achieving schools providing base for competitive economy and inclusive society
3 Schools for a knowledge society	• Development of ICT and the National Grid for Learning • Community learning centres • Lifelong learning	Schools as learning communities equipping students for: • job retraining • lifelong learning • personal fulfilment

Source: Adapted from Caldwell and Spinks 1998, p. 11

Notice board 1   Top–down and bottom–up change – why both?

◆ Few organisations, if any, are now wholly autocratic – the private fiefdom of those who run them.

◆ A case for change may be made from outside the school or the education system, or from within.

◆ Whether the initial impetus is driven internally, externally or in partnership, individuals will start from different perspectives about the desirability of the change and the nature it should take.

Notice board 1   Top–down and bottom–up change – why both? (cont.)

◆ The inspiration/impetus for change may come from a variety of sources – the designated leader; a motivated individual; organisational consensus; the efforts of a determined minority; the actions of a committed majority; within-school, local, regional or national networking; or multidimensional influences.

◆ There are many obstacles to change. For example: what the change may look like when complete may not be clear, thus uncertainty may lead to concerns and tensions; many people have a natural resistance to change along the 'not done here/tried before' continuum; the change may require 'unlearning' or the acquisition of new skills; the change may have to be achieved with limited or reduced resources, and there may be more than one way to proceed.

◆ Professional relationships and institutional dynamics will be very significant. Contractual mandate, consultation, negotiation, obtaining co-operation, motivating interest groups, steering clear of conflict, and sustaining internal and external impetus will all be necessary.

For all these reasons and more, a two-way flow will probably be more successful than pressure from one direction alone.

Strategic PIN down – Reflection 1.1	**Aims** ◆ to examine potential areas of tension between school outcomes (Track 2) and learning outcomes (Track 3); ◆ to identify school-based solutions that meet the requirements of both tracks.

P – State the PROBLEM	In our relentless pursuit of exam results, we are in danger of . . .
I – Clarify the ISSUE	To provide an imaginative curriculum which will stimulate the pupils and achieve . . .
N – Tackle the NEED	To develop teacher confidence in their ability to . . .

Strategic
PIN down –
Reflection
1.1 (cont.)

Before you begin, think about:

◆ How good are your exam results? Would they be better if (a) there was a greater focus on creativity; (b) if teachers were really encouraged to try things out and take risks?

◆ Do you know if teachers in the school feel a tension between what they want to do and what they think they have to do? How could this issue be explored productively?

◆ Has the school narrowed its curriculum to accommodate the government agenda? Think of practical alternatives to what you have in place.

Tip
Gather specific examples from within and outside the school where teachers have used creative approaches to promote effective learning – for example the infant school where, as part of literacy hour, the children eat the alphabet as nibbles and print it on stones in the playground.

Conflict over values

'Industrial relations are like sexual relations. It's better between two consenting parties.'

Vic Feather

Change is more likely to be particularly stressful when it involves a threat to our own values and beliefs, since it is these which give our lives a sense of meaning and purpose. Government has sought to raise standards by engineering a power shift from the producer to the consumer that is safeguarded and regulated by the state. The 1988 Education Reform Act set up a quasi-market where school budgets depended on pupil numbers and pupil numbers depended on parental choice. As the players in the marketplace, schools would need to compete with each other for pupils, with the competitive spur acting to drive up standards. Business values, predominantly concerned with survival in the marketplace, have come into conflict with public service values, whose main concern is to meet the needs of the community as a whole through collaboration, collegiality and the exercise of professional autonomy. Specifically, within the educational setting, this means meeting the needs of each individual and developing her/his potential.

The post-1988 imperative for survival has increased the pressure on schools to consider, and in many cases take up, courses of action that will benefit their own institution at the possible, probable or inevitable expense of other schools in the neighbourhood. Pull measures designed to attract parents of the more able, better motivated children – thereby creaming them off from the local pool – have included the adoption of grant-maintained status, the introduction of a measure of selection or 'specialist status' and, within the school, setting arrangements. Push factors include playing down special needs provision for prospective pupils and more readily getting rid of pupils with behavioural problems, with both groups of pupils likely to end up in the low status, low performing schools with falling rolls and spare places. According to Gewirtz *et al.* (1995), the logic behind such measures is clear:

> 'Filling up a school with "able" children and keeping children with SEN [special educational needs] to a minimum is the cheapest and most labour efficient way of enhancing league table performance.'

pp. 185–6

Issues in focus 1.1

What role, if any, should the market have in education? The two views presented below are from different ends of the ideological spectrum and both are critical of the 1988 settlement.

Let's choose catchment area, not market force

School A is marginally better (or at least perceived as such by parents) than school B. Word gets around. Year by year, school B loses pupils and money; school A gains. School B becomes quite a bit worse: it has to reduce staff (and, therefore, the range of subject specialisms); it delays repairs, redecoration and the replacement of textbooks.

The reasons to choose A rather than B, once marginal, become significant. Increasingly, the children who go to B are reluctant conscripts. The world being what it is, they tend to come from the less motivated, less clever, less prosperous families. Good staff flee; morale plummets. The poor intake starts to show up in exam results. Parents who once would have accepted B as a tolerable, if second-best, alternative to A will now move heaven and earth – and go right through the appeals system – to keep their children out of it.

In other words, parental choice, far from raising standards, has created a bad school where previously there was a decent, if not a brilliant, one. And more parents are more dissatisfied than they ever were before . . .

May I dare to suggest that we abandon the market in education and go back to catchment areas? And that, in designing such areas, we require local authorities (remember them?) to 'have the greatest regard to' . . . the need for every school to have a balanced ability intake? . . .

The more sensible parents will realise that a school is nearly always good when it has a balanced intake.

Wilby 1997

Better choice than producer whim

Wilby worries that choice leads to more 'sink' schools . . . but . . . subjecting producers and suppliers of consumer goods and services to the rigours of genuine competition does not lead to failing enterprises limping along, perpetuating disadvantage for those who have to patronise them.

The market is too unkind for that. It is not that there are no failing restaurants, say; simply that they cannot exist as failing restaurants for very long. There is no reason why the same consideration would not pertain in the education market.

But notice where this argument is leading. It is precisely that we should follow the 'market to its logical conclusion' – which is much further than current reforms have taken us. Away with the state regulation of the curriculum and teaching force, away with state provision of schooling.

Tooley 1997

Grace's study (1995) of 88 primary and secondary headteachers from the north-east showed that most were concerned about the new value conflict and its impact on their work. They were particularly worried that:

> 'the managerial preoccupations of headteachers would distance them from the pupils, the experience of direct classroom teaching, collegial relations with their own staff and colleagues in the locality. This was a concern expressed particularly by women headteachers.'

Grace 1995, p. 74

In the competitive situation of the marketplace, headteachers are much less likely to share good practice, openly admit to school problems, such as drugs or bullying, or seek help from each other in time of need, thereby cutting off a particularly valuable source of help during stressful periods.

The conflict over values has been experienced by many teachers on a day-to-day basis within their own classrooms. What is of value to most teachers, and what therefore motivates them, is making a difference to the lives of the children they teach, opening up their minds, helping them grow and develop. What is publicly measured, and therefore officially valued, is the number of pupils they get through a particular examination hoop or who reach a particular National Curriculum level.

When teachers perceive that (a) their capacity to make a difference through their own teaching is diminished, whether as a result of overload of marking and preparation, the need to cover the syllabus and teach to the test, or the marginalisation of creative, low status subjects and (b) their efforts in the above area are not recognised and valued within the school and/or society at large, then their job satisfaction declines along with a sense of their own self-worth. The point is made tellingly by a primary school teacher who explains why she is leaving her post:

'Over the last 2–3 years I have become more and more disillusioned with the teaching profession. It used to be a job I adored and found totally fulfilling. However, it is now more about statistics, SATs [standardised assessment tests], league tables, targets and paperwork, and sadly the child has become lost in the middle of all this. Also, teachers' professionalism, autonomy, creativity and freedom has gradually been eroded to such an extent that it is impossible to act as an individual. There is no longer the time to spend with children to develop proper relationships.'

Hutchings *et al.* 2000, p. 114

Challenge to culture

'I intended to give you some advice but now I remember how much is left over from last year unused.'

George Harris

Government reform has deliberately challenged teachers' professional culture – their ingrained habits, their ways of working and their relationship with colleagues. Teachers in England, despite experiments with open plan learning, have been accustomed to work on their own as autonomous professionals. Once they had survived external observation during teaching practice and their probationary year, teachers were seldom disturbed within their own domain of the classroom. There they have plied their trade, operating in the description of Evans (1996) as:

> 'independent artisans, autonomous tinkerers and intellectual craftsmen',

p. 235

with the effective practitioners developing their craft knowledge and skills through their own experience of what works and what doesn't.

This habit and practice has come under frontal assault from successive governments, each determined to force open the classroom door in order to improve the quality of teaching. The main battering-ram has been OFSTED, first through the inspection process of observing, judging and reporting on the standards of each teacher and, second, in applying pressure on heads to set up rigorous internal systems to monitor and evaluate teaching. There has been a lot of mostly quiet and covert resistance to this in schools. Some has come from headteachers concerned that:

> 'classroom teachers will see such observations as threatening and . . . good staff relationships will suffer'.

OFSTED 1998a

Some resistance has come from heads of department in secondary schools, reluctant to exercise critical judgement in respect of their colleagues' work and thereby disturb the comfortable and congenial cultures that have often existed in schools alongside the culture of individualism. Many classroom teachers, especially the older ones, have also resisted observation, concerned that it may question their competence and require them to change age-old habits.

The second battering-ram used by the government has been appraisal and performance management. The first assault, in the form of appraisal, launched by Sir Keith Joseph, largely failed to disturb the classroom defences. Most schools found they either didn't have the time or subverted the process into a comfortable conversation focusing on the teacher's strengths and her/his own professional development needs. The second assault, via performance management, appears to have closed down the escape routes. How it will be applied in schools remains to be seen. The topic is discussed in more detail in Chapter 8.

Issues in focus 1.2

Many reform programmes have failed because they did not take account of the organisation's culture. The term culture has been defined by Schein (1985) as:

> 'the deeper level of basic assumptions and beliefs that are shared by members of an organisation, that operate unconsciously, and that define in a basic "taken-for-granted fashion" an organisation's view of itself and its environment'.

p. 6

Thus, the character or culture of a school will be represented in large part by 'intangible' but nevertheless real characteristics, such as its value system, the general tone around the place, the standards it chooses to recognise and reward, its ingrained working habits, the conduct of its staff and pupils (and the 'unwritten' rules such conduct presents), the quality of personal and professional relationships, and the overall educational ethos, by which everyone 'recognises the place', even though they may not be able to describe the ethos in exact terms.

Work on school culture by writers such as Stoll and Fink (1996), Fullan and Hargreaves (1992) and Evans (1996) have identified some key points that are helpful to school leaders considering how to manage change in a way that wins the consent of the staff:

◆ The prevailing culture of an organisation has a profound impact on how people respond to change.

◆ Culture tends to be a strong conservative force, since radical change threatens existing culture. People may pay lip-service to change but carry on behaving in the same way as before.

◆ Expressions of culture reflect preferred ways of working, for example: 'we are used to working on our own while enjoying a friendly relationship with our colleagues', or 'we prefer to be told what to do', or 'we prefer working together, sharing ideas and acting as critical friends towards each other'.

◆ Organisations tend to have predominantly positive or predominantly negative cultures, for example: 'we believe we can make a difference and we work hard to improve', as opposed to 'the odds are stacked against us and there's nothing we can do'. However in schools, like all organisations, there are often different cultures at work, sometimes in conflict with each other.

↓ ◆ Before embarking on change, school leaders should seek to (a) identify the existing culture or cultures; (b) think about what culture they wish to establish; (c) make use of existing culture, where helpful; (d) ensure change strategies include personal modelling of desired behaviour; (e) encourage opportunities for stakeholders to reflect on and discuss culture and values; and (f) identify specific situations where intervention is likely to have a positive effect on shaping the culture.

Strategic PIN down – Reflection 1.2

Aims

◆ to reflect on the school's existing teacher culture and its current arrangements for monitoring teaching;

◆ in the light of that analysis to consider the best ways of encouraging teachers to benefit from classroom observation.

P – State the PROBLEM	When teachers are observed teaching, they often feel . . .
I – Clarify the ISSUE	To provide valuable feedback that is welcomed by the teacher and enables her/him to . . .
N – Tackle the NEED	To create a system and climate which enables teachers to develop and provides head and governors with . . .

Before you begin, consider:

◆ What arrangements are currently in place for observing teaching? What purposes do they serve? What effect do they have?

◆ Are the arrangements hierarchical or do they include opportunities for peer observation? What are the pros and cons of running both approaches?

◆ How are these arrangements viewed by teachers? How would you describe the existing teacher culture in the school? Do teachers talk about their work with each other informally and formally at staff/department meetings?

◆ How you would present the case to the teaching staff for having a system of classroom observation in place that meets the need you identified?

Tip

Think about the value of a group of volunteers whose remit is to investigate good teaching, carry out some classroom-based action research and report back to the rest of the staff.

Pressure and support

'You only have power over people so long as you don't take everything away from them. But when you've robbed a man of everything he's no longer in your power – he's free again.'

Alexander Solzhenitsyn

Successful change generally needs roughly equal amounts of pressure and support. The perception of most teachers is that the pressure far outweighs the support. There is intense pressure on schools to perform. Each year the issuing of results coincides with parental choice of school. Each year the school is under pressure to improve its performance and meet higher targets. Headteachers, accountable to the governors for school results, have transmitted the pressure down the line, establishing formal line-management systems of internal accountability.

The support has been less in evidence. Financially, the percentage of national income spent on education (4.7% of GDP in the 1997–2001 Parliament) is below the OECD average and, according to Emmerson and Frayne (2001, p. 5) 'actually lower than the 5.0% achieved by the Conservatives in the [previous] Parliament'. As a result of planned increases this is forecast to rise to 5.3% in 2003–04. Politically, teachers have been held responsible for 'the school problem', first characterised as left-wing egalitarians and woolly liberals and, more recently, as conservative Luddites resisting modernisation. Locally, within schools, the vital support of parents and children has become more conditional, more problematic and generally, it would seem, less forthcoming. Rapid technological change has been accompanied by social fragmentation, as evidenced in the fact that 28% of children will have experienced divorce in their family before the age of 16 and in a threefold increase in child poverty since 1979, with one in three children living in families with less than half the average income. The result is that many children are less able and willing to concentrate, listen and learn. More children, according to two researchers in this area, Norwich *et al.* (1999):

'are arriving at nursery school and behaving in aggressive, frightening and sometimes violent ways'.

This situation is made worse when the pressure to drive up standards leads to a narrow curriculum and pedagogies that fail to take account of the needs and starting point of the learner.

In an age when the consumer rules, parents are more prepared to make demands on teachers and challenge their authority. At its worst, in more middle-class areas, this can, in one teacher's experience, take the form of:

Hutchings *et al.*
2000, p. 158

'very pushy, demanding parents [who] would come storming into the classroom saying why haven't you done this? why haven't you done that?'

In deprived areas, it is more likely to take the form of violence or verbal abuse against heads and teachers. Pressures facing teachers in deprived areas are particularly acute. This is partly because the areas themselves have become more deprived with both 'the flight of the respectable working class to middle class home ownership' (Toynbee 1998) and an increase in poverty. It is also partly due to the effects of the 'market revolution', which has led in some schools to concentrations of pupils with low socio-economic status, making the job of the head and teachers particularly challenging. This is vividly illustrated in Gewirtz's study (1998) of two contrasting secondary schools situated within a mile of each other in inner London. At Beatrice Webb, 30% of the pupils were refugees, 30% on the special educational needs register and 70% eligible for free school meals. The school experienced falling rolls, poor exam results and low staff morale. The head and the teachers spent much of their time managing and controlling pupils and dealing with incidents related to behaviour. At Ruskin school, just over 20% qualified for free school meals and 15% were on the special educational needs register. The school was oversubscribed with good exam results and high staff morale. Teachers had more time and energy to spend on developing the curriculum and taking part in extra-curricular activities. One teacher said:

Gewirtz 1998,
p. 450

'we're really looking at the curriculum all the time. [We] spend very little time worrying about disciplining classes.'

School leadership

Charles Handy
and Robert Aitken

'There is a certain pleasing conceit among most of us that any sensible person can handle individuals or groups if they need to. Thus it is that people are launched into being parents with no warning or training and into management with a similar careless confidence.'

With the intense demands of the centralised reform programme, the quality of school leadership has become critical in influencing how teachers feel about their work, whether they remain as teachers and how well they do their job. In London, where on average there are only 4.2 applications for each primary headship post, a survey carried out for the Teacher Training Agency (TTA) (Hutchings *et al.* 2000) showed that poor school management was the main professional reason for teachers leaving their posts. Forty-five per cent cited this as a reason to leave. In the experience of one teacher:

> '[The] head teacher made a series of very poor managerial decisions. In one year, [the head] overspent the budget, victimised a member of staff and had no understanding of setting or implementing the school development plan . . . the will to go for the children and parents is TOTALLY knocked out of you.'

Hutchings *et al.* 2000, p. 112

For many of those leaving it was the combination of poor management and the impact of the government agenda that led to their decision:

> 'The workload was sixty plus hours a week. This did not work out as a parent . . . the head gave me one term to become a good teacher. He felt I had not done so and almost gave me no other choice but to leave. His philosophy, for example, that reception children must **always** work in total silence, and mine simply did not mix. His withdrawal of support coincided with the penultimate day of the OFSTED inspection at the end of my first term. I was simply too exhausted to argue. There was no support for a severely handicapped child who entered my class with severe learning difficulties.'

Hutchings *et al.* 2000, p. 107

Evans's study (1998) of the attitude of nineteen primary school teachers to their work found the educational vision and management skills of the head were key factors in motivating staff and giving them a sense of job satisfaction. Teachers with a clear educational vision of their own were particularly demotivated when the head's priorities were not about children's learning but rather about, for example, avoiding conflict or maintaining administrative efficiency:

Evans 1998, p. 109

> 'she'll check the record books, and she'll check everbody is where they should be . . . but the actual content of what you're doing . . . I don't think she bothers one jot.'

Heads who did not recognise and value what committed teachers were doing and achieving, often in difficult circumstances, had a very negative impact on morale:

> 'I think it was the lack of recognition that really bothered me, that whether I do it or don't do it, he doesn't think any different of me . . . in my classroom, he's never once come and said "Oh, that looks a good piece of work you've done with the children." '

Evans 1998, p. 134

So far, we have looked at why there is a serious problem of low teacher morale and job satisfaction. A government agenda that intensifies the workload at the same time as it reduces teacher autonomy places particular demands on school leaders. The analysis in this chapter provides some initial pointers for school leaders about how to respond to these demands in a way that encourages staff to give of their best in difficult times:

- avoid a localised replica of the top–down model;
- promote discussion and exploration of issues in the area of value conflict;
- influence and shape a collective vision, centred around educational purpose;
- recognise and respect existing teaching culture, particularly when seeking to change aspects of it;
- balance individual staff needs and aspirations against team targets and performance;
- ensure that new teachers, teachers new to the school and teachers with leadership potential receive effective mentoring, training and development;
- demonstrate a positive commitment to staff development;
- utilise all the internal and external support that is available;
- focus on essentials in order to reduce overload.

We will explore these pointers, along with other ideas and approaches, in later sections of the book.

Interesting facts 1   Locus of control

There is no sign that increased centralised control, more government initiatives, and increasing accountability will decline rapidly or cease. Nor is there concrete evidence that their cessation would bring only benefits. The combined effects of the central agenda may be a reduction in recruitment and a reduction in those willing to seek headship, or the system may settle to less turbulence and teachers will feel more secure as they revive their influence. Whatever the outcome, school leaders may find it helpful to discuss with individuals and teams where they perceive 'locus of control' to be and how they might change an overly negative disposition into something more positive.

◆ Rotter (1966) distinguished two cognitive styles related to the evaluation of performance. Some people adopt an internal locus of control, focusing attributes of their performance to qualities within themselves; others prefer to look outwards seeing an external locus of control as primarily responsible for their performance. Put differently, internal locus sees outcomes as contingent on personal actions; external locus holds tight to the view that environmental or external happenings determine what success or satisfaction one achieves.

◆ Lefcourt (1991) argues there is no general locus of control factor that can predict behaviour, but specific locus of control scales are better (those tailored to specific professions or social groups).

◆ Though Kline (1993) does not see hard pyschometric support for a locus of control behavioural construct, general observation would suggest that people do tend to sway predominantly in one way or the other in ascribing blame for professional and/or personal actions. The tendency to take either course of action to extremes may on the **internal** scale lead to resignation or ill health, and on the **external** scale to the belief that 'I can do nothing – they are in control'. Thus it is important for staff to discuss expectancies and beliefs about all levels of control in order to determine what specifically it is they can do something about:

> 'perceived self-efficacy – the belief that "I can do it" – is a foundation for the successful pursuit of a difficult goal or for changing and improving one's situation or oneself. Its psychological opposite, perceived helplessness, is the route to giving up, apathy and depression.'

Mischel 1999, p. 472

Of course, not all direction is a bad thing. There may be a psychological need for some aspects of control (Buchanan and Huczynski 1985) since by various types of external order people get systematic structures, feedback and degrees of comfortable dependency. However, good leaders, competent managers and confident employers know that they do not necessarily lose power or influence by delegating fairly to those who are nearer to the issue in question, or to those who have key responsibilities for seeing that aspirations become actions.

Summary

Ralph Waldo
Emerson

'When the eyes say one thing and the tongue another, a practised man relies on the language of the first.'

◆ Successive governments have applied intense pressure on schools to raise standards.

◆ The result has been to raise pupil attainment, but, as a result of the methods used, this is at the overall expense of teacher morale and job satisfaction.

◆ The government programme has been imposed from the centre; it involves a significantly increased workload for teachers; it conflicts with the dominant values and culture of many teachers within the profession; and it is generally seen by them to provide too much pressure and insufficient support.

◆ Government reform of schools has happened at a time when the impact of change in the wider society has made it more difficult for teachers to win over the support and co-operation of parents and children. This problem is particularly acute in schools serving disadvantaged communities.

◆ The central programme has placed immense demands on school leaders: they have to meet the requirements of the external agenda, take staff with them and stay true to their own personal values and vision.

◆ The quality of leadership is the key factor at local level which influences and affects teachers' attitudes to their work.

◆ Analysis of the causes of the problem of low morale and job satisfaction point school leaders towards some possible ways of responding to the demands and pressures.

◆ Personal perception of where control lies is the most important influence on response. It is important to appreciate what one can self-regulate and develop.

Overview

It is often said that people are the most important, most creative and most expensive resource that any organisation has. It is equally true that they can be both trying and troublesome. Many school leaders and team leaders are frequently heard to remark 'it's not the kids who take up my time, it's the staff' or something similar. This is not surprising, as being able to deal with 'people potential' and 'people problems' is the true heart of applied leadership and management. Of course, there are no guaranteed remedies, no quick-fix solutions and no 'yellow brick road' to take us over the rainbow. All designated leaders have to come to understand the people who work with them and how best to make the most of their interests and skills. This often means dealing with ambiguity, changing behaviours, a catalogue of personal and professional needs, and the effects on people's work of their lives elsewhere. In general, the vagaries of human nature present the most puzzling and the most difficult tasks that confront the school leadership team. The upside is that many people often surprise us with their sustained enthusiasm, imagination and diligence in the face of very challenging circumstances. This chapter begins to look at some of these aspects of the people equation. It starts with a reminder that other organisations and professions tackle similar issues and that the people-element includes working with a range of stakeholders. It provides some attention to the issues of people as a resource, understanding their motives and securing their commitment. It concludes with some consideration of leadership styles and how these may influence staff response. Some of these issues are picked up in other parts of the book, as indeed they are right across the series.

Sharing perceptions and working with stakeholders

> 'Just as doctors' and vets' mistakes die, managers can kill their organisations. We can learn from others . . . yet be discriminating about what we allow to cross the learning bridge.'

Everhard and Morris 1985

Schools, perhaps taking their cue from the school improvement industry, tend just to look at themselves and each other when examining how to manage change in challenging circumstances. However, there is much to learn from studying other organisations, from both the public and private sectors, that have achieved success by bringing out the best in the people who work for them. There is a huge databank of material and experience to draw on as well as some innovative ideas. This can be very useful, provided we continue to bear in mind the differences between both sectors over purpose. Businesses are primarily concerned with profitability and survival in the marketplace: success is easy to determine. Schools are concerned with educating people and enabling them to develop. As Bottery (1992) puts it:

p. 113

> 'You want an articulate, enterprising, flexible, sensitive individual as an end product? When does someone become this?'

With this caveat in mind, there is a large area of common ground: all organisations consist of people with goals, ambitions and a desire for self-fulfilment, working with others to achieve some common objective within a framework designed to get the most out of them. Recently more ground has become common as:

◆ business has come to recognise that people, not systems, are at the heart of organisational success. What makes the critical difference in the post-industrial economy is the knowledge and ideas of the people who work for the company, rather than its finance and technology as in the past. Schools, of course, have always been about people and the learning that pupils acquire through their interaction with the teacher;

◆ schools are operating in a new climate of accountability to their stakeholders, familiar to business, and have to demonstrate they are performing well by national criteria and whatever other criteria have been agreed locally with the stakeholders.

Notice board 2   The stakeholder labyrinth

We need to look after all key stakeholders, keep balance in the time and energy distributed between them, be aware of their principal aspirations, interests and concerns, and work with them on strategic and more immediate issues. Every school needs to take stock of who their key stakeholders are. So, who are the key stakeholders in your school?

Notice board 2   The stakeholder labyrinth (cont.)

Students, parents, governors, teachers, representatives of local education authorities (LEAs)/trust bodies, central government, teaching support staff (internal), teaching support staff (external), residential care staff, administrative, catering and technical staff, union officials, feeder schools, further/higher education institutions, parents, families, volunteers, local community officers, careers service advisers, medical/health and safety personnel, employers, accreditation agents (e.g. from examination boards, youth award ventures, proficiency schemes), partnership link staff in other schools – including any overseas.

Management issues to consider with regard to stakeholders will include:

◆ purposes for links;
◆ reciprocal expectations/responsibilities;
◆ relationships;
◆ key roles and responsibilities;
◆ main arrangements for liaison/communication;
◆ shared aims;
◆ joint working;
◆ actual or potential disagreements.

A continuing central question will be: What more can we do to promote a sense of common commitment and endeavour?

Issues in focus 2.1

From their study of America's best-run companies, Peters and Waterman (1982) concluded their success was due to their application of the following eight principles. Which of these, do you think, are particularly relevant for schools? Are there any that aren't?

1 **A bias for action** – a preference for doing something – anything – rather than sending a question through cycles and cycles of analyses and committee reports.

2 **Staying close to the customer** – learning his preferences and catering to them.

3 **Autonomy and entrepreneurship** – breaking the corporation into small companies and encouraging them to think independently and competitively.

4 **Productivity through people** – creating in **all** employees the awareness that their best efforts are essential and that they will share in the rewards of the company's success.

5 **Hands-on, value driven** – insisting that executives keep in touch with the firm's essential business.

6 **Stick to the knitting** – remaining with the business the company knows best.

7 **Simple form, lean staff** – few administrative layers, few people at the upper levels.

8 **Simultaneous loose–tight properties** – fostering a climate where there is dedication to the central values of the company combined with autonomy and scope for innovation.

People as a resource

Dr Vernon Coleman

'Whatever else you try, and however much you spend on high technology equipment, nothing will improve your company's efficiency and profitability more than taking care of your employees, reducing their exposure to stress and learning how to get the best out of them. Your company's biggest hidden asset is the people it employs.'

Geoffrey Morris

'A show of strength is a fairly normal reaction to being underestimated or taken for granted.'

What the evidence from all types of organisation shows is that how people think and feel about their work strongly influences how much extra they are willing to put into their jobs and how well they do them. The think-well/feel-good factor is more likely to occur when:

◆ the organisation makes genuine efforts to secure an integrated approach to both strategic and day-to-day issues;

◆ people's own values and vision are in tune with those of the organisation and these are clearly centred around notions of fairness and justice and belief in human potential;

◆ the values of the organisation are expressed by and experienced through the systems and processes it operates and by the way people behave towards each other;

◆ the organisation has a positive, identifiable culture, which, amongst other things, encourages people to work together and share ideas;

◆ the organisation devotes time to motivating, valuing, challenging and trusting staff, and getting the different relationships right;

◆ effort is expended to establish effective communication, including encouraging openness, consultation and reflective listening;

◆ the general operating ethos is that no individual is given authority without responsibility, and never given responsibility without authority;

◆ individuals feel they have a part to play in achieving organisational success and that part is recognised and rewarded;

◆ the part they do play involves meeting challenges by exercising initiative, taking responsibility and making decisions within their area of work;

◆ individuals have the opportunity to grow and develop as a result of feedback and coaching.

Understanding motives

> 'What comes from the heart, goes to the heart.'

Samuel Taylor Coleridge

When organisations are making these things happen, they are responding to what motivational theorists, such as Abraham Maslow, Frederick Herzberg and David McClelland, have identified as the key influence that drives our behaviour – that of fulfilling needs. Once basic survival requirements, such as food and shelter, have been met, what then motivates people are (a) social needs, such as the need to belong, to be recognised and to exert influence over others; (b) needs relating to oneself, such as the need to achieve, to develop and fulfil oneself.

McClelland's (1987) explanation of motivation is particularly convincing as it is based on detailed, empirical observation of how people behave. He found that three motives account for nearly 80% of our social behaviour, both in work and outside it:

◆ the need for achievement (the drive to do something better, either than other people or than our own previous best);

◆ the need for affiliation (the drive to maintain warm, close relations with people and avoid conflict);

◆ the need for power or influence (the drive to exert influence over others, either by making others weak and dependent (personalised power) or by making others strong and independent (socialised power)).

According to McClelland, we each have our own motivational profile, formed early in life and difficult to change. This makes us better suited to some jobs rather than others. Successful salespeople, for example, need to have a high achievement drive. Their satisfaction comes from achieving better sales figures. Those in teaching will often have a high achievement and socialised power drive, the latter concerned with the satisfaction of helping children become independent and able to think for themselves. Those in teaching with a predominantly affiliative drive may find it more difficult to exert classroom control and, in a leadership role outside the classroom, take unpopular but necessary decisions because of their need to avoid upsetting people.

Schools should, therefore, seek to appoint teachers with appropriate motivational profiles and create an organisational climate that enables them to satisfy their motivational drives. This includes:

◆ setting challenging tasks with specific feedback on how well the individual has done;

◆ providing opportunities for all teachers to exercise leadership roles outside the classroom;

◆ recognising and developing the leadership role that all teachers play within their classrooms.

School leaders need to pay particular attention to factors that enable teachers to do their core job better – teaching children and in the process satisfying their needs. These include minimising bureaucracy, avoiding overload and creating a self-disciplined approach to learning which permeates the school.

Issues in focus 2.2

In a seminal paper printed in the *Harvard Business Review* in 1976, McClelland and Burnham outlined their view of what motivational profile makes a good leader. This summary includes McClelland's postscript, added in 1995:

◆ Successful managers have a strong need for power, that is influencing others so that they can become strong and responsible. This need has to be disciplined and controlled so that it is directed towards the benefit of the institution, not towards the manager's personal aggrandisement.

◆ Successful managers of smaller enterprises, in particular, need a strong achievement drive that shows itself in a constant concern for improvement.

◆ Managers motivated by personal power are not good institution builders. Their subordinates tend to be loyal to them, not the institution. Hence disorganisation often follows the departure of the leader.

◆ People with a strong affiliative drive tend to be poorer managers. Because they want to stay on good terms with everyone, they often make exceptions to rules, which others resent as being unfair.

◆ It is not intelligence that separates the best people from the worst when it comes to performance. People who scored exceptionally well on the Scholastic Aptitude Test, which measures aspects of IQ, often function poorly as managers. What separates world-class leaders from mediocre ones are specific behaviours such as self-control, self-confidence, an ability to get a consensus from people, and strong motivation for achievement and/or power.

Securing commitment

'You drive a car and the car takes you where you want to go. You do not drive a plant to grow. Nor do you drive a teenager. Nor do leaders drive their organisations (or teams). The school is a living system like the plant and the teenagers. There is no one driving it. You tend a plant to grow and you need to tend a school or a team.'

Peter Senge

The central task of the leader, whatever the organisation, is to create a vision for that institution that excites the enthusiasm and secures the commitment of its members. Commitment brings energy, perseverance and ideas and is therefore crucial to organisational success. But it is not easily obtained, and several things need to be in place before it is.

Personal values

> 'One looks back with appreciation to the brilliant teachers, but with gratitude to those who touched our human feelings. The curriculum is so much necessary raw material, but warmth is the vital element for the growing plant and for the soul of the child.'

Carl Gustav Jung

Organisational vision is shaped, although not exclusively, by the leader's own vision, which in turn derives from their own personal values. According to Starratt (1995), the vision of educational leaders is:

> 'always based on assumptions and beliefs about the nature of learning, about the essence of being human, about the nature of human society, and about the purposes of schooling'.

In a recent study of twelve successful schools, the team (Day *et al.* 2000) found that the headteachers all drew on a core set of personal and professional values – including a fundamental respect for others, a belief in each person's potential and a capacity to trust others – accompanied by a strong sense of integrity, fairness and honesty in relationships with others. The values and vision had a moral force, concerned with the betterment of others, as opposed to an instrumental view that sees education as a means to an economic or social end. And, crucially, the vision was shared, securing commitment, not compliance, as, in the words of Senge (1990):

> 'a shared vision is a vision that many people are truly committed to, because it reflects their own personal vision'.

p. 206

Behaviour and integrity.

'A person's work is a self-portrait.'

Anonymous

For the organisational vision to have meaning, people need to see both the big picture and the detailed brushwork that shows their part in its realisation. Clarity is the *sine qua non* but by itself does not eliminate scepticism nor engender commitment. The leader's own behaviour, and that of the leadership group, will strongly influence the extent of trust and therefore commitment. That behaviour is subjected to microscopic examination and forensic analysis wherever stakeholders gather together. Do the leaders deeds match up to their words? Do they actually believe in what they say? Do they treat people with respect, actively listen to what they say and value what they do? Do they have integrity and can they be trusted or do they tell different stories about the same thing to different people? Are their values, beliefs and actions consistent with each other? If the vision is about realising each child's potential and the leader has her/his own set of favourites amongst the teachers to whom she/he pays particular attention, then the vision is tarnished, the leader's credibility undermined and trust will not be forthcoming.

Systems and processes

> 'It is sometimes a bit of a shock to be reminded that, in operational and practical fact, the medium is the message.'
>
> Marshall McLuhan

Values also need to be embedded in the organisation's systems and processes if commitment is to be long term. Two important areas are communications and performance management. One of the essential skills of contemporary leadership is the ability to provide authoritative direction while encouraging ideas and initiative to flow upwards. If the organisation does value its members, what opportunities are there for them to contribute their voice and views? In the best tradition of Adam Smith, self-interest reinforces ethics. As Heller (2000) points out:

> 'In all companies, rich veins of knowledge, know-how, initiative and willingness run from top to bottom. Unless the blood flows both ways, companies will lose the future that could have been.'

Strategic PIN down – Reflection 2.1	Aims
	◆ to review the flow of ideas and information within the school;
	◆ to consider what changes are necessary to ensure that ideas and information flow in both directions.

P – State the PROBLEM	To get through the crowded, demanding agenda, school leaders often use a . . . approach to the management of change.
I – Clarify the ISSUE	In dealing with the problem, the issue is to avoid going to the other extreme . . .
N – Tackle the NEED	The need is to have processes in place that provide direction, while enabling . . .

Strategic
PIN down –
Reflection
2.1 (cont.)

Before you begin, think about:

◆ where the school is in the top–down, bottom–up continuum;

◆ the strengths and weaknesses of the current arrangements;

◆ what direction you think the school needs to move in;

◆ what needs to happen to make the change work – think of a specific situation where a new approach could be tried and what you need to do to make it work.

Tip

Think of an example where grassroots experience either has had or could have had a beneficial effect on the way change was managed.

Performance management is another key area where practice needs to reflect values. Here the important issue for an organisation is whether the way it manages the performance of each individual enables that person to develop her/his potential and, in the process, helps to secure organisational success. Experience of successful practice shows that:

◆ Individual objectives need to be in alignment with organisational objectives, with individuals clear on how they can contribute to organisational success and in what way they have contributed.

◆ There has to be regular discussion about the interdependence of individual and school development so that individuals recognise how best to work in teams to fulfil 'whole school' aims.

◆ The atmosphere has to be one of mutual support, focused on achieving greater staff effectiveness and appropriate pupil progress.

◆ Individuals have to be involved in identifying and planning their development needs and opportunities, and this practice has to be part of a long-term sequence of professional review and development.

◆ 360-degree feedback needs to be in place – with managers, peers and those the individual manages providing feedback that covers how the person behaves towards others as well as what she/he has achieved. This type of feedback, which needs to be regular and ongoing, draws attention to discrepancies between how we see ourselves and how others see us and is thus an essential tool for personal development and organisational effectiveness.

◆ The main focus throughout the process needs to be on personal development, with the manager moving from the role of 'cop to coach'.

Targets need to be agreed, not imposed, as the process is about 'dialogue and mutual commitment' (Turner 1998).

◆ The issue of linking performance with pay needs to be handled carefully. The extensive research study on performance management carried out by the Institute of Personnel Development (Armstrong and Baron 1998) showed that where pay review was linked directly with performance review, the developmental aspects of performance management were seriously prejudiced:

> 'Most organisations felt that the weaker the link between performance management and PRP (performance-related pay) the better it was for both processes, and the more likely they were to have a positive impact.'

p. 122

Measuring commitment

> 'Everyone sees what you appear to be: few experience what you really are.'

Machiavelli

To secure commitment, organisations need to measure it. Otherwise it gets neglected. Companies such as the computer firm Hewlett-Packard use both 'hard' measures, which examine performance, and 'soft' measures, which look at attitudes, in conjunction with each other. They know from their own experience that high levels of trust, pride in the organisation and commitment lead to high levels of performance. Over the past ten years, the company has achieved an average annual growth rate of 20%, and regular surveys of attitudes show consistently high levels of trust, pride in the organisation and commitment running at over 80%.

In her study of successful international companies, Gratton (2000) found that a critical element of their success was their ability to secure the commitment of the workforce. Hewlett-Packard has achieved this through a very distinctive culture, 'the HP way', which reflects the core belief of its founders back in the 1940s that:

> 'men and women want to do a good job, a creative job, and that if they are provided with the proper environment they will do so'.

Peters and
Waterman 1982,
p. 244

The belief in everyone's ability to do well is signalled in Hewlett-Packard's company practice:

- there is no fast-track system;
- the profit-sharing reward system is open to everyone;
- flexible working arrangements make it as easy as possible for people to look after children or ageing parents;
- regular problem-solving sessions are open to all and opportunities to pursue new ideas are funded;
- senior managers are selected for their enthusiasm and their ability to engender enthusiasm in those they manage.

Within this value system, the company sees its main task, in the words of one of its senior managers as of:

Gratton 2000
p. 82

> 'creating a stretching context and environment which will allow people to flourish and grow'.

It achieves this through what Gratton describes as 'a subtle combination of the "soft" and the "hard".' The hard element is 'the relentless focus on growth and profitability'; the soft element is 'the value set that places dignity and respect for the individual employee at its centre'. Both elements are at work in the performance management process: challenging targets aligned to corporate objectives are the hard element; the soft element is the freedom of the individual to determine how to meet the targets and how to use the personal training budget allocated to them. Everyone is clear about both corporate and individual goals and performance, through weekly reports on company performance and informal day-to-day appraisal of individual performance by team leaders.

Leadership styles

John Macbeath

> 'Effective leadership may depend on from where it is viewed or what social and psychological set of preconceptions one brings to it.'

Studies of managers worldwide have shown that the styles of leadership they use have an important effect on how people feel about their work, which in turn affects their performance and the performance of the organisation. Recent research carried out by Hay/McBer (Goleman 2000) found evidence of six particular leadership styles, each of which had a distinctive effect on the climate of the organisation, and each of which was appropriate in particular circumstances:

◆ **coercive style** ('Do what I tell you') gives orders and insists on immediate compliance;
◆ **authoritative style** ('Come with me') creates long-term vision for the organisation and persuades others to follow;
◆ **affiliative style** ('People come first') creates harmony, focusing on the positive and avoiding conflict or confrontation;
◆ **democratic style** ('What do you think?') builds commitment by establishing consensus and involving people in decisions that affect their work;
◆ **pace-setting style** ('Do as I do now) sets high standards for performance through personal example;
◆ **coaching style** ('Try this') enables people to develop by giving feedback on performance and encouraging long-term goals.

The research found that each style had a measurable effect on each of the six dimensions that make up the organisational climate or working environment. These dimensions are:

◆ **flexibility** – the extent to which people feel able to innovate without being held back by rigid rules and systems;
◆ **responsibility** – the extent to which people are given responsibility for carrying out tasks and feel accountable for the outcome;
◆ **rewards** – the extent to which accurate feedback on performance is given, with good performance recognised and rewarded;
◆ **standards** – the extent to which challenging, yet attainable, goals are set and insisted on;
◆ **clarity** – the extent to which people can say what the organisation's values, vision and priorities are and what their role is in bringing them about;
◆ **team commitment** – the extent to which people pull together as part of a team.

The main conclusions of the research were:

◆ Leadership styles affect the organisational climate, and this has a significant effect on organisational performance.
◆ The authoritative leadership style has the most positive effect on climate. The affiliative, democratic and coaching styles also have an overall positive effect on climate, whereas the coercive and pace-setting styles have an overall negative effect. However, these two styles are

required in certain situations where, for example, disciplinary action needs to be taken or tasks need to be finished quickly.

◆ Successful leaders are able to call on and make use of a range of leadership styles according to what the situation requires. Less effective leaders often rely on one or two styles they feel comfortable with.

Strategic PIN down – Reflection 2.2	**Aims**

Aims
◆ to review your use of leadership styles;
◆ develop ways of extending your range.

P – State the PROBLEM Leaders often stick with the leadership styles they are comfortable with, applying them in situations where they may not be . . .

I – Clarify the ISSUE The issue is to develop self-awareness and confidence in this area because . . .

N – Tackle the NEED The need is to be able to use a range of leadership styles effectively so that . . .

Before you begin, think about:

◆ what styles you make most use of and why. Is it because the situation requires them, or is it because you are most comfortable with them?

◆ a recent situation in which you used a particular style that was appropriate and effective, and another situation where the style was inappropriate and ineffective. In the latter situation, what style would have been more appropriate? What do you need to do to feel confident about using that style effectively in a similar situation in the future?

◆ how you can get feedback from those you work with about the styles they think you use. Are their perceptions different to yours? If so, what do you think are the reasons?

◆ the context of your school. Does its situation need you to develop leadership styles you are not making much use of?

Tip
Involve others you work with in this reflective activity and encourage them to consider their own leadership styles. If you are members of the leadership group, does the group itself make use of the full range of styles?

Interesting facts 2   Women as leaders

For some people it is an anathema to divide leadership qualities or leadership styles along gender lines. Others suggest that there are perceptible differences between women and men in how they lead and manage and that to understand these is to benefit the professional development of both sexes. For example, it has been suggested that a more focused study of how women lead organisations and manage staff could help to rectify the under-representation of women in senior management, as well as offer alternative approaches to those men who see people management as something of a macho sport.

Some key facts about women as leaders and managers:

◆ Historically speaking, apart from a few icons – whose leadership exploits may be based more on myth than on reality – women have had to overcome the 'deficit notion' to take on leadership responsibilities. In broad terms, there have been two interpretations of 'deficit'. First, that women were not born to lead, and therefore simply could not do it. Second, though they could assume a serious leadership mantle, to do so successfully meant they had to learn to be 'more like a man'.

◆ Both directly and indirectly, the acceptability of women in leadership may also have been undermined for both genders by (a) the preponderance of androcentrism in academic and practitioner writing about leadership and management practice and (b) the lack of specific exemplars of women as heads, or as other team leaders, in published case studies of schools at work.

◆ Other commentators have pointed to a raft of influences on both under-representation and a fair reporting of impact. These influences include societal, institutional and organisational ideologies, role or career restrictions and sex segregation (see, for example, Martin *et al.* 1983; Davies 1985; Jayne 1989).

◆ More recent enquiries have centred around developing a pedagogy in professional training that is more centred on the contributions and achievements of girls and women, plus the development of a research praxis centred more vigorously on challenging inequalities in education (Weiner 1994).

◆ Evidence from case studies, other action-based research and semi-structured interviews with teachers (collected as part of survey or inspection activities) presents female leaders as being:

    ◆ less confrontational in style;
    ◆ less abusing of power;
    ◆ willing to work more energetically and consistently at participative leadership;

- better acquainted with professional behaviours that support other teams (e.g. curricular leadership, pupil support strategies, parental liaison and resource management);
- more concerned about the quality of pupils' learning and the professional performance of teachers than several male colleagues tend to be;
- able to adopt a style that encourages staff to change, rather than one that is directive.

Some general implications of gender in school leadership that need to be taken into consideration by both female and male team leaders include:

- monitoring equal opportunities in day-to-day practice;
- examining the causes and nature of any school factors that unfairly constrain women's advancement along the leadership path;
- ensuring that women have fairness in opportunities that prepare for the leadership function – for example, staff mentoring; leading school teams or sectors of the school; sharing expertise with others generally and/or in the role of advanced skills teacher; holding responsibilities relating to the governing body, staff appointments and liaison with external agencies; and work related to the school development plan and performance management;
- helping others to change negative perceptions of, or inappropriate responses to, female leadership;
- acknowledging and supporting effective examples of leadership from both genders and also rewarding those who recognise it and contribute to it.

Summary

J. Murphy

'Leaders have to lead not from the apex of the pyramid, but from the centre of the web of human relationships.'

- Schools can learn from other organisations that operate successfully in a demanding environment and get the best out of their staff.
- Successful organisations, whether public or private, tap into people's own values and vision, satisfy their motivational drives, capture their enthusiasm and secure their commitment.
- This commitment comes through a compelling organisational vision, born out of the personal beliefs and values of its leaders, rooted in a belief in human potential and high ethical standards, lived out through the actions and behaviour of the leaders, and embedded in the organisation's systems and processes.

◆ Successful leaders have a positive influence on the organisational climate, and thereby its performance, by making use of a range of leadership styles appropriate to the particular situation.

◆ All leaders need to consider gender issues. For example, schools – through their culture, curriculum delivery and their allocation of team responsibilities – have much to contribute to improving life chances for girls and women.

Overview

In this chapter we examine six case studies of individual schools where the headteacher's leadership and management of staff has resulted in high morale and strong collective performance. The schools cover the age range 3–18 and include inner-city primary and secondary schools serving disadvantaged communities as well as schools with more socially balanced intakes.

Whatever the phase or social context, all the schools have made significant progress in terms of the quality of education they provide for their pupils. This progress is directly linked to the way the heads have led and managed a collective response. Evidence of progress comes from OFSTED reports, examination results and interviews with the headteacher and a small representative sample of staff.

The case studies do not attempt to tell the whole story behind the head's success in leading and managing change; instead we focus on one or two themes that emerge from our analysis as being critical to understanding the approach adopted in each school. The names of the schools and heads are fictitious, the descriptions are not.

School recovery: Ridgeway Community School

'If the creator had a purpose in equipping us with a neck, he surely meant us to stick it out.'

Arthur Koestler

Ridgeway Community School is a mixed non-selective 11–16 school with 670 students. It is in an area where 30% of the local school population attend grammar schools. Forty per cent of the school's pupils have special educational needs and a significant minority have behavioural difficulties. Twenty-four per cent are entitled to free school meals, 2% are from minority ethnic backgrounds and 1% have English as an additional language.

The 1997 OFSTED inspection found the school to have serious weaknesses. In particular it was noted that:

◆ results in external examinations were poor;
◆ absence rates were high;
◆ student behaviour was frequently a cause for concern.

Since then a new head, Ken Fogarty, has been appointed. Ken was previously a deputy at the school. As a result of his programme of improvement, the 2000 OFSTED inspection noted:

◆ a 'remarkable recovery' in a very short time;
◆ exceptionally effective leadership;
◆ much good teaching;
◆ general effectiveness and no significant weaknesses.

The dramatic turnaround in the school's performance has been largely due to the influence of the new head. He is driven by the belief that all children can do well, a belief that was shaped by his own experience of being bottom of the remedial class in a secondary modern school. The turning point for him came when his metalwork teacher, who had no idea he was not doing well in other subjects, told him that the work he was doing was brilliant. Spurred on by this praise, Ken went on to become head boy and gain six O levels:

> 'It's quite simply things like that which have affected the way I think and the way I've got the staff to think and believe in the kids here. I say to the children in assembly there is no reason why the so-called slowest and least able among you shouldn't be standing where I'm standing today in 30 years' time.'

Ken's first task was to persuade staff and students to abandon expectations of underachievement and failure and replace them with the conviction that everyone can and will achieve and that the school could and would be outstanding – 'the best in the county'. The school, in effect, made its own fresh start: it had a new name, a new uniform, a new motto ('Strive for Excellence') and its own core values – 'Co-operation, Challenge and Work'. The focus of the school is very much on learning. A notice in the entrance says: 'Beyond this point learning is the most important thing we do.' This message is reinforced through assemblies, staff development days, monitoring arrangements, the rewards system and virtually every area of school activity.

Ken has paid particular attention to securing a talented and committed teaching force, without which he knows the motto and values will remain on paper. He made it clear to teachers and classroom assistants that everyone had a vital role to play and there was no room for obstructers or people not fully signed up to what the new school stood for. He has recognised, valued and rewarded, where possible, teacher skill and commitment; he has confronted teachers whenever their behaviour has undermined the school's purpose. One long-serving teacher at the school said the effect of the new head had resulted in 'a quantum leap in my own professional development'. He now saw what the school could achieve and he believed in his own ability to help make that happen. Others felt uncomfortable with the new regime and left. Nearly half the teachers have left the school since the new head was appointed, seven as a result of some form of disciplinary action.

Selection procedures for the appointment of teachers are rigorous, designed to ensure that the successful candidate is the right person for the school. All short-listed candidates are asked to teach 'their best lesson' to a particular class, and they are observed by the head, the senior teacher responsible for staff development and a governor. At a subsequent interview, Ken makes a point of asking questions designed to tease out the candidate's resilience and her/his capacity to deal with difficult situations in class.

Stemming from his own early experience of school failure, Ken Fogarty has put in place structures and teaching strategies that are designed to maximise the chances of every learner being successful. There has been an effective drive to promote literacy in all areas of the curriculum. According to OFSTED, the special educational needs (SEN) department makes excellent use of its army of learning support assistants, both for withdrawal and for 'providing crucially important support in many lessons to students who would otherwise not be contained in mainstream classes'. The head uses staff development days to promote enquiry and debate about effective teaching and the characteristics of a good lesson. Teachers have examined how they can cater for all learning styles and how they can accelerate learning by creating the conditions for high challenge through the use of open-ended questions, while sustaining low stress through effective classroom management. Expert practitioners on the staff are used to demonstrate good practice. The enquiry and discussion has resulted in agreed school strategies in such areas as:

◆ differentiation;
◆ the design and content of schemes of work;
◆ the layout and use of lesson plans.

Each department is monitored once per term over a period of two weeks: in the first week, the head of department (HoD) observes each member of the department teach; in the second week, the leadership group carries out the observations. One teacher commented that her teaching had improved because 'I am no longer flying by the seat of my pants'.

The leadership group, consisting of the head and three senior teachers, demonstrates what Peters and Waterman (1982) call 'the hands on, value-driven approach' to leadership. They have a visible presence around the school. They are finding out what is going on and whether the school is doing what it says it is doing. They are picking up areas that need attention and they are reinforcing good practice, often through immediate praise of both staff and pupils in front of others. They are providing a model of behaviour for others to emulate. As well as forging a highly effective senior leadership group, Ken has also succeeded in creating a dynamic leadership group amongst the heads of department; eight of the twelve have been appointed since he took over. Their primary task is to use their skills and initiative to achieve the desired transformation within each of their departments.

Ken makes use of a range of leadership styles, according to their particular relevance. In his own words, 'sometimes I tell; sometimes I listen'. His use of the **authoritative style** was graphically illustrated at the start of his headship when he held the first-ever whole school assembly in the sports hall to tell the students and the staff that from now on this was a new school with a new ambition, and he depicted what the students could expect and what would be expected of them.

He frequently makes use of the **democratic style** in conjunction with the authoritative style. The school motto and the core values came out of a staff development day when the staff and governors discussed in groups 'what are we here for?' This took place after the assembly at which the head outlined his vision for the school. Following the recent OFSTED report, on other development days teachers were asked to come up with ideas, via house team discussion, for three areas identified as needing improvement:

◆ enhancement of learning;
◆ student attendance;
◆ partnership with parents.

The senior teacher responsible for staff development makes particular use of the **coaching style**. In the last academic year he met with all teachers by November to discuss their own short- and long-term development needs and their role in meeting the particular needs of the school before agreeing targets, that reflected both needs. Ken made more use of the **coercive style** at the beginning of his headship when he was rooting out poor practice and unacceptable behaviour. For example, the first sample of exercise books collected from two departments to monitor the new marking policy revealed that only one member of staff had carried out this policy. Ken summoned all members of both departments to his room the following morning and told them that their failure was unacceptable as it had let the students down. He informed the rest of the staff what had happened. Subsequent monitoring has shown that the policy has been followed consistently.

Developing a climate of confidence: Stow Cross Primary School

> '*Nil desperandum*. Upon the wreckage of thy yesterday . . . design the structure of tomorrow.'
>
> Anonymous

Stow Cross Primary School is an inner city school housed in an attractive new building. It has 209 pupils on roll. Thirty-seven per cent are eligible for free school meals, 21% have special educational needs, 61% belong to minority ethnic groups and 40% have English as an additional language. The head, Catherine Turner, has been in post for eleven years. The 1997 OFSTED report described Stow Cross as a 'good school with some outstanding features . . . the headteacher is a strong and effective leader whose vision has established a clear direction and purpose for the school. She is ably supported by the staff team.'

The school now is very different from the one Catherine took over eleven years ago, when it was sited in two separate gloomy Victorian buildings. The teaching staff of nine was dominated by four teachers who called themselves 'the senior teachers'. They had the best classrooms, the best timetable and their own toilet. When the head tried to introduce new ideas, she was met with 'we've always done it like this' or 'well, what can you expect with children like ours?' They lodged complaints about the head to the new chair of governors, appointed after the head had taken up her post. The chair, described by the head as 'a misogynist with a mental illness', orchestrated a vendetta against her that was designed to remove her from her post. 'He wouldn't speak to me in public, was rude and abusive about me in governing body meetings and wrote letters of complaint about me, sometimes posting them through my letter box in the early hours of the morning.'

Looking back on the early days of her headship, Catherine said: 'I don't know why I became head here. I didn't read any of the signs. I supposed that I wasn't experienced enough!' But she refused to give in and eventually forced the issue to a tribunal, which found in her favour. The chair of governors and the whole governing body were removed. Two of the 'senior teachers' left within six months.

This whole period lasted for four years. What kept Catherine going was her resilience, combined with her vision of what the school could become. This had been influenced by her own childhood experience. She came from a working-class family in Ireland from whom she had acquired a passion for learning, as 'everyone talked about everything around the table'. This was in stark contrast to the poverty of her education, which she recalls as being dominated by 'nuns and tedious lessons'. Despite gaining a university place at 16, which she didn't take up, nobody told her that she was talented and could make something of her life. She passionately believes that every child is talented and every child has the right to a good education that will enable her/him to make the most of their talents. She is particularly drawn to teaching working-class children, many of whom she sees as trapped in a cycle of deprivation with poor language skills and low self-esteem and expectations:

'My message to them continuously is about raising their self-esteem, making them feel good about themselves and telling them they are unique and exceptional. I tell them to go out in the world and make a difference. It's a great privilege for me to be involved with these children when I know that I am making a difference.'

Catherine gave herself four years to transform the school after the departure of the governors and some of the staff. The challenge remained formidable. During the four years of turmoil, the low educational standards she had inherited had further declined. The new governing body and the LEA still thought the head was at least part of the problem. She was visited every week by an LEA inspector, who set her tasks to do and targets to meet.

The first task she set herself was to persuade the staff 'what we can do with our children'. She worked to build up the staff as a team, initially through vision-building activities that asked them why they went into teaching, what they wanted the children to achieve and what their vision for the school was. She extended the process to include support staff, children, parents and governors, asking them what they wanted the school to become. The staff then spent two days looking at their collective approach to discipline and children's behaviour:

> 'There were some very hot cups of coffee and I warned staff not to touch them. Quite a few of them did touch the cups. I then used this as an example. If we say to children 'don't do that' they are likely to do it, as we all are. We need to change the way we say things to them.'

The staff explored better ways of promoting good behaviour. The policy was rewritten with an emphasis on the positive. The 'don'ts' and raised voices were consigned to the past.

Armed with school improvement research material from an MA course she had begun to study, Catherine told the local authority that their constant monitoring was ruining her efforts to turn the school around. The weekly inquisitorial visit stopped. Through her assemblies, her teaching and the way she interacted with everyone in the school she modelled the vision. A member of the non-teaching staff commented:

> 'Catherine is a very caring person and is sympathetic to everyone's needs. She tells you how well you are doing and asks for your opinions, for example about whether the children should be called for lunch instead of having to queue. You know with her the children come first.'

Catherine also invites feedback on her own performance. She asks the children to critique her assemblies and say what they have learned from them. She sends out an annual letter to parents and staff asking for comments on how well she is doing and areas she can improve on. She acts on the feedback. A generally shared view was that she was good on ideas but not so good on follow-up and consolidation, as she was always wanting to move on to the next idea. Reflecting on this, she turned the key stage units into school improvement teams, whose prime purpose was to stick with the agenda of monitoring the progress of the pupils at their key stage in order to raise standards. She has made it clear that she welcomes people raising concerns or voicing criticism: 'I want them to let me know, so we can do something about it.'

The school has now established the practice of all teachers receiving constructive feedback on their performance. This began through the head's own example and as a result of her intelligent handling of a sensitive issue. The teachers were initially suspicious of being observed teaching. The head made the point that the experience would prepare them better for inspection. She used a colleague from the local university to establish teacher confidence in classroom observation. The colleague worked with the teachers for a year on a scheme to identify, disseminate and share good practice. It started with the literacy hour. The literacy co-ordinator taught an exemplar lesson that she described as 'not brilliant, but how I would do it'. She was observed by all four colleagues teaching the key stage, plus the consultant who critiqued the lesson, while the head took the other children for an assembly. Each teacher subsequently invited the co-ordinator and the consultant in to observe one of their lessons. The feedback session began with the teacher's own thoughts about how the lesson had gone.

With numeracy, the co-ordinator used the key stage meeting to identify areas where the children were weak before opening up discussion on what the teachers felt were their own strengths and weaknesses. Later she produced a matrix that showed that the areas where the teachers felt least confident were generally the areas which the children found most difficult. Discussion then followed about how best to tackle those areas. The numeracy co-ordinator taught an exemplar lesson which, as with the literacy lesson, was critically analysed. The teachers, who had enjoyed a positive experience with the literacy feedback, volunteered to teach a lesson in front of two observers in an area of the curriculum that they found difficult. They discovered that the preparation, the teaching, the feedback and the discussion were an extremely valuable way of improving their own teaching. The head attributed the recent 'dramatic improvement' of the results of the SATs to this collective approach. The collaborative exploration of effective practice has given teachers the confidence to open up their own teaching to constructive feedback in a way that has helped them to improve. The co-ordinator gave feedback to the head about the lessons she had observed, providing firm evidence that the quality of teaching was high. Additional support was sensitively given to one teacher where it was needed.

The climate of confidence has also been helped by the head's encouragement of teachers not to fear failure but rather learn from it. She uses staff meetings to report back to staff on aspects of good practice that she has noticed when observing lessons. In one situation, she observed a newly qualified teacher (NQT):

'The lesson went disastrously wrong. She had a lot of children with special needs. She had over-planned the lesson and lost track of the situation. I told her not to worry. "We won't count this one. We'll have chat about it afterwards and I'll come and see you another time." Afterwards I told her that I hadn't realised what the demands were and arranged for an extra assistant to help her. The following week at the staff meeting, I said: "We've got a very brave teacher. The lesson I was watching went haywire. We had a good discussion about it afterwards and Linda invited me back for another lesson which went really well." '

In general, Catherine makes full use of all the leadership styles, discussed earlier, that are needed to sustain the school's long-term performance. Through her use of the **authoritative style**, staff know what the school stands for and are aware of the importance of their work, individually and collectively, in making the school a success. **Coaching** through feedback is used to promote professional development. The **affiliative style** is very much in evidence. There are lots of social gatherings that are attended by teaching and non-teaching staff, and the head communicates with a card or flowers if significant illness strikes. The **democratic style** is demonstrated by the head's passionate belief that everyone has the right to have a say in how the school is run. The OFSTED report commented that 'a significant strength of the leadership and management is the collegial approach to decision-making' which 'extends to the pupils, whose opinions are listened to with respect and often acted upon'.

Creating a school of excellence: Forest Oak Secondary School for Girls

Ralph Waldo Emerson

'The reward of a thing well done is to have it done.'

Forest Oak is an 11–16 girls, Catholic, inner-city comprehensive school with 782 pupils. Ten per cent of the pupils have special educational needs, 21% are entitled to free school meals and 20% are from minority ethnic backgrounds. The headteacher, Martha James, has been in post for nearly ten years. She took over a school where pupil behaviour, attendance and examination results were poor. Since then, the school has become an oversubscribed Beacon School with outstanding examination results. It was described by OFSTED in 2000 as a 'school of excellence', where 'excellent leadership has created a positive and supportive ethos in which pupils show a thirst and enthusiasm for learning'.

When Martha took over the school, she met all the teaching staff individually, as well as the pupils, parents and governors. She asked them:

◆ what they valued about the school;
◆ what they saw its strengths and weaknesses to be;
◆ what they wanted the school to become.

What emerged was that people liked the way the previous head did things, but couldn't identify clearly what the school stood for. Martha then proceeded to work on a mission statement that reflected her own beliefs and those of many of the people she interviewed. The mission statement has served as a living document, which is continuously used to:

◆ reinforce the ethos of the school;
◆ inform the work of the school and the priorities for development, including the curriculum and how teachers teach;
◆ sustain how people relate to each other and work together;
◆ reflect on practice, as different aspects of the mission statement are reviewed every year by staff and pupils to see whether they are being realised.

The heart of the mission statement reflects Martha's belief that education is about 'bringing people to life', enabling them to acquire a sense of dignity and self-worth; to be highly aspiring and develop confidence in their own ability to think for themselves and deal with situations; to demonstrate a concern for others and express that concern through action. These beliefs stem from her own religious conviction that 'every child is part of Christ and has its own giftedness'. The school is enabling each girl to become 'more fully human and thus closer to God'.

Particular emphasis is placed on two aspects of teacher behaviour, seen as crucial to realising the mission statement:

◆ The first is the way teachers treat and relate to pupils. Stemming from Martha's driving belief in each individual's inherent self-worth, there is an insistence that all members of the school community treat each other with respect. Teachers are expected to apply rules firmly and fairly, avoiding at all times the use of humiliation and sarcasm. The leadership group both models expected behaviour and challenges unacceptable behaviour from whatever source. When, for example, the deputy head came across a member of staff who had lost his temper and was shouting at a pupil, he helped to deal with the immediate incident and then shortly afterwards spoke to the teacher in private. He found out what had happened, pointed out that the teacher's behaviour was not appropriate and went through how to deal with the situation in a better way.

◆ The second aspect of teacher behaviour relates to the quality of teaching. The classroom, laboratory or workshop is where teachers can and do 'bring pupils to life'. They have the opportunity to be moral transforming agents, and the responsibility to carry out that role. In every subject the curriculum is designed to challenge the pupils and to develop independent thinking. The science and mathematics departments use CASE and GAME, curriculum programmes designed by researchers at King's College, London, to develop thinking skills. All departments have started to build into their schemes of work opportunities for pupils to work in their own preferred learning styles. This development had its origins in the Religious Education department and provides an instructive example of how good ideas can spread and take root in a collaborative environment where local initiative is encouraged. The head of the RE department went on a diocesan course, 'not normally a great deal of fun'. This one was. It was about accelerated learning and learning styles. She enthused about it to the deputy head who was in charge of staff development. He encouraged her to go on another course about accelerated learning led by Alistair Smith. In her words:

'It was fabulous. I raved about it for weeks. I got our year 7 pupils to do a questionnaire that enabled them to find out their best learning style and we started to develop and use materials which suited their different styles. Other people got interested and we shared a lot with other departments with whom we had good links. In the summer I went on a bizarre and fascinating course on brain gym. Later on, four of us, encouraged by the deputy, started a MA course which also looked at accelerated learning. The more I got into this, the more excited I became. Our other deputy who teaches RE encouraged other heads of department to use similar approaches through her line-management meetings. When it looked like it needed some overall co-ordination, a focus group was set up with members from each department to share ideas and avoid duplication.'

There is a strong emphasis on the observation of teaching, both to ensure that standards are high and to enable teachers to develop and improve. The process begins when a new teacher is appointed. Each candidate has to teach a lesson. Those who pass are then interviewed by the deputy head, who provides feedback on the lesson, assessing their responsiveness to constructive advice. The quality of teaching, the capacity to improve and the commitment to the school's mission statement are the three key criteria for appointments.

Teachers are observed teaching on several occasions each year as part of appraisal and departmental reviews. The deputy head responsible for staff development observes everyone teach at least once a year. Lessons are judged good, satisfactory or unsatisfactory, with verbal and written feedback provided. By observing everyone, he is able to gauge overall strengths and weaknesses of the teaching and thereby identify areas for improvement that may need a whole-school focus. He is also able to develop his role as coach, using the follow-up session to provide feedback on observable strengths and possible areas for development and to open up a dialogue about potential routes to self-improvement. One member of staff, in her second year of teaching, commented on how this had helped her to improve:

'I think that my general approach to questioning has developed quite a lot since I have been at the school. If someone gives a wrong answer, I am no longer saying, "No, that is wrong" and asking someone else. Now I am more likely to ask two or three questions of the same pupil, maybe encouraging her, rephrasing the question,

> giving some clues. Feedback from the deputy after he had observed my lesson helped me here. He said "Don't always stop at one question. You may want to follow it up." This point was reinforced later on an INSET day when the trainer said that a lot of teachers fall down on this and only ask one question. If it is the wrong answer, they don't pursue it. You also have to have the confidence to do this. When I was a student teacher I thought that unless someone gave me the right answer, the lesson was going to fall apart.'

With this overview, gained from observing all the teachers, the deputy sometimes suggests that a teacher observe somebody else teach who is particularly strong in the area identified as needing improvement.

The leadership group principally uses three leadership styles. Martha makes use of the **authoritative style** to emphasise the importance of the mission statement as the touchstone for all the school is doing and to remind individuals of their significance in helping to bring this about. She also makes use of the **coercive style** when she perceives that teacher behaviour is obstructing the school's purpose of 'bringing people to life'. Martha used this style extensively in the early days when she moved quickly to establish new systems and ways of doing things. This included a rigorous appraisal scheme based on systematic lesson observation. Staff left if they were uncomfortable with the new approach and/or were unable or unwilling to meet its requirements. Martha applied competency procedures to three teachers. Half the teaching staff left within two years, including both deputies. Martha continues to make use of both authoritative and coercive actions when teachers are seen to be letting pupils down. 'Let me be very clear about this' is likely to be followed by 'let me be very direct' if the required change of behaviour is not forthcoming.

Extensive use is made of the **coaching style**, particularly by the deputy head when feeding back to teachers on lessons observed. The culture of the school is very much about continuous improvement at the institutional and individual levels. The philosophy is that institutional improvement cannot take place without individual improvement.

Less use is made of the **democratic style** of leadership. Improvement ideas and initiatives are driven from the top where the leadership group initially discusses them. Any proposition may be floated at middle-management meetings to:

- gauge responses;
- identify difficulties;
- work out trade-offs.

Individual line-management meetings may be used to influence possible doubters and further test and refine a specific proposal before it is presented to the whole staff.

Through thinking to action: Walpole Infant School and Nursery

Anonymous

'Acting without thinking is a bit like shooting without aiming.'

Walpole Infant School and Nursery has 214 pupils aged 5–7 plus a 60 place nursery unit. It is in a mixed suburban area that contains private, council and rented accommodation. Seventeen per cent of the pupils are entitled to free school meals, 20% are on the SEN register and 6% come from minority ethnic backgrounds. On entry, the attainment of pupils, according to the recent OFSTED report, is 'broadly in line with the national average'. By the end of Key Stage 1 the attainment of pupils in English, mathematics and science is 'well above the national average'. The inspection report describes the school as 'very successful . . . The head effectively leads the school in a continuous quest to improve the standards of education for the pupils. She is very well supported by the enthusiastic deputy head and the hard working staff.'

The head, Mary Roberts, has been in post for eight years. She has a clear view of the qualities she wants the children in the school to develop and demonstrate:

- confidence;
- a good work ethic;
- questioning and decision-making skills.

The importance she attaches to questioning and decision-making derives, in part at least, from her own experience. She was brought up in a single-parent household in a tough council estate in Liverpool. She went to a high-achieving primary school where the expectation was that the children would go on to the local grammar school, although that was a rarity in her neighbourhood. Having got to grammar school, she was the only one in her class from day one in a second-hand blazer; she was also the only one to be harassed and shouted at on the street corner when she returned home in her uniform carrying a satchel. The only books in the house were Arthur Mee's encyclopaedias. She joined the local library at the age of 6, read the first book she took out the same afternoon and brought it back, only to be told that she had to have it out for at least one day. She gained a place to university, but nearly didn't take it up:

'At one point I said, I don't think I'll go to university. I can't afford it. My mother said, "That's fine if that's what you want". In the end I only went because the headteacher stepped in and said, "No, you can't not go". The school gave me a loan to get through the first three weeks until the grant came through. Without that support I would have sunk without trace. That is why I am so passionate about children being given the opportunity to make choices and to realise they have choices to make.'

She was told to study zoology at university because that was her 'best' subject at school. She did so, even though she would have preferred to have studied production management:

'Although a bit of a freethinker, I always accepted what I was told. There are times when it would have done me good to query if that was the only way of doing something.'

Mary encourages everyone at the school to query things and to ask the question why. In the classrooms the emphasis is on teachers stimulating the children's curiosity so that they also ask the question why. Staff meetings have been used to discuss strategies for asking the pupils open questions and restricting the use of closed ones. Teachers plan their work in year groups to include open questions, brainstorming activities and knowledge webs. These approaches are used to find out at the start of a topic what the children know, what they don't know and what they think they need to know. Mary makes use of assemblies to ask the children questions and come up with answers they can apply. For example:

'In a recent assembly I told the children that we have a problem with lots of crisps being left on the floor under the tables. I asked them how and why we have this problem and what they thought we could do about it. They came up with various suggestions – such as not sitting close enough to the table, putting too many crisps in the mouth at one time – in the light of which they then undertook to deal with the problem.'

The head uses this questioning approach with staff, and indeed with all stakeholders, to move the school forward. How can we improve the school? And with staff: How can I develop and improve my skills, knowledge and capabilities? Mary has a good picture of what is happening in the school. She often goes into the open-plan classrooms, taking visitors around or informally observing for ten or fifteen minutes. She welcomes people coming to see her with what may be ideas, problems or concerns. One member of staff commented:

> 'If you have got a good idea, Mary wants to hear it. She'll make you feel good about yourself and support you through it.'

Another member of staff observed:

> 'Mary is very approachable and interested in you as a person. I can go and see her with a problem and know that I will be listened to. I also know that I can trust her.'

The head has created a collaborative problem-solving climate where staff feel secure about identifying problems they may be experiencing. They feel confident about putting forward their own ideas for improvement. Staff meetings are used to brainstorm new initiatives and decide ways to improve on existing practice.

For example, the school was one of the first to develop its own approach to teaching able children. This came out of teachers raising concerns about what they should do to ensure that able children learned in line with their potential. The issues was discussed at a staff meeting. In addition, Mary went on a course, and then ran a workshop looking at practical classroom approaches. Out of this work came the policy that set up a 'talent register' and identified specific classroom strategies to use. For example, children who were able in a particular area might cover the same work as the others, but approach it differently by being given a list of answers and asked to work out what the questions might be.

All members of staff are encouraged to ask themselves: How can I improve and develop? They are encouraged to undertake training that will enable them to do so.

At all job interviews candidates are asked: 'Tell us about the worst day and the best day you have had in the classroom.' This is designed to explore their capacity to reflect on themselves, their classroom practice and their ability to learn from both success and failure. Staff are encouraged to use their initiative, to risk failure and develop confidence in their own ability. One newly appointed teacher copied the teaching approach of two colleagues in the same year group. She said:

'I realised it wasn't me. I felt awful and got very upset. I went to see the head. She told me that I didn't have to do it like that. "Do it how you want to." I just needed someone to say that. She had the confidence that I would get it sorted out.'

The question Mary asks all staff is "What are you doing next?" During the year, each teacher has four days of non-contact time, part of which is used by them for their own professional development. One day is for work in their own subject area (each teacher has responsibility for at least one subject area); one day is for writing reports and assessments; one day is for work in the area of the classroom, which may involve observing somebody else teach, visiting another school or looking at an aspect of pupil management; and one day is to go on a course of their choosing.

Training opportunities are open to all, and staff are expected to take them up. The senior nursery nurse has been at the school for fourteen years and has seen her job change from being pot-washer and sweeper-up to having an important role in enabling children to learn. This includes being involved with:

◆ teachers in planning work;
◆ writing individual education plans;
◆ preparing appropriate learning materials;
◆ helping groups and individuals who need extra support.

Mary knows from her own experience that many talented adults have not been able to make the most of their potential in terms of qualifications and jobs. Quick to identify the nursery nurse's capabilities, she arranged for her to go on a HND Specialist Teachers' Assistants course at the local university. The nursery nurse commented:

'Confidence-wise, the course gave me a tremendous boost. I can go into a classroom and a teacher may say to me, "I've got a child who is having difficulty with this. I've tried all these ideas. What can we do?" I might say, "Give me until tomorrow. I'll have a think and see what I can come up with." '

The nursery nurse has also developed an expertise in supporting children with specific learning difficulties. She uses this to good effect in the classroom. The head encouraged her to go on a year's part-time course because she knew of her interests in this area of SEN.

Mary has also built up an excellent team of midday supervisors (MDSAs) who play a vital role in managing the behaviour of the children at lunchtime. She described how she had done this:

'Midday supervisors are difficult to recruit, but having got together a team I set out to build up the self-esteem of the group and raise the profile of the job. I appointed an intelligent and caring MDSA and sent her for training in first aid and managing challenging behaviour. We had daily briefings before lunch to update her on children causing concern. I gave her a budget to choose new uniforms in agreement with the others. The other members of the team were offered options on a rota basis and began to ask, "When is it my turn for training?" I allow them odd days off (without pay) to take up cheaper holidays within school time. Staff meetings are held after lunch once per term and problems are raised with me. I now have a committed team and a list of people wanting to join! The importance of backing up the team and then working with staff and not against them cannot be stressed enough. The benefits can be seen in a vast improvement in playground behaviour.'

Mary applies her questioning to the government agenda, asking to what extent it is helping to improve the quality of education and raise standards. Through observation and discussion with staff, she is clear that the National Curriculum is 'overloaded and too prescriptive'. The consensus is that the numeracy hour is well thought out and working well, but the literacy hour has serious flaws, particularly with respect to extended writing. Following discussion, the school decided to modify its approach: the hour is less than an hour, teachers do not follow the carousel of five activities, and once a week the literacy hour is replaced with a session on extended writing. Any querying of this by the LEA or others has been met by referral to the SATs' results. Mary's assertion of the individuality of her school represents the approach of many successful heads: they have the self-belief to adapt the government's agenda to the needs of their own school rather than let it dictate their actions.

Mary makes extensive use of all four leadership styles associated with long-term performance. She has succeeded in achieving a genuine **collaborative** culture where all staff are working together to create a caring environment in which the children flourish and learn. In a cramped school where the head's tiny office is close to the overcrowded staff room, the head is in frequent contact with staff on an informal basis. Mary uses this opportunity to establish **affiliative** relationships that operate within a framework of shared understanding of what everyone is trying to achieve. Through her use of the **authoritative style**, teaching and non-teaching staff are clear on their particular role in making the school a success and feel their own commitment and contribution are recognised and valued.

Mary uses the **democratic style** to gain insight and ideas into how to make the school better and strengthen the sense of team commitment. She uses the **coaching style** extensively to promote the long-term development of all members of staff. Although there is little formal observation of teaching (she is concerned about the possible effects on collegiality of the formal requirements of performance management), through her frequent visits to classrooms she has a good knowledge of each teacher's strengths and areas for development. These are discussed at the annual interview. After an informal visit to the classroom she may talk to the member of staff about something she has observed, which might be related to lack of rulers in the classroom or a particular child who may be causing a problem. If any observation suggests criticism of the teacher's approach – for example, the use of questions – she will raise the issue at a future staff meeting as a general aspect for consideration by everyone. She feels this collegial approach is best suited to a small organisation, characterised by friendly, informal relations and strong individual and team commitment.

Modelling and developing professional competence: Bridge Market Junior School

Johann Wolfgang
von Goethe

'Correction does much, but encouragement does more.'

Bridge Market is a junior school for pupils aged between 7 and 11. It has 330 pupils on roll who come from a wide range of socio-economic backgrounds. Five per cent are eligible for free school meals, 16% have special educational needs and 3% speak English as an additional language. The headteacher Annie Speight, has been in post for twelve years. She took over a school with a privileged intake. It was seen to be doing well in the local area but she considered it as 'coasting'. In particular, it was not bringing out the talents of the working-class element of the school population. Indeed, these children were regarded by some teachers as the underclass. One teacher had told a parent whose child had learning difficulties that 'someone has to collect my rubbish and be my dustman'.

Annie's attempts to change the culture were met with resistance. 'It was hell for two years', she said. 'I felt the knives in the back.' She worked closely with the local inspector who knew the school well. Annie met the teachers individually to discuss their careers and future plans, encouraging some to raise their sights and go for promotion. At the start of her headship she observed that 'because of the prevailing culture, it wasn't possible to observe staff teaching', so she asked the inspector to observe three teachers whose classroom practice she was concerned about. The inspector insisted that the head was present at the feedback, where areas for improvement were identified together with a programme of support. By the end of the year the three teachers had left. After the departure of one of them Annie noted that 'the staffroom changed overnight and stories emerged about how this teacher had reduced some of the younger staff to tears, telling them that they weren't any good'. The 1999 OFSTED report found that the 'headteacher and her senior colleagues provide very good leadership and are constantly striving for improvement in every aspect of the school'. It went on to state that 'staff have positive attitudes, act as a team and provide very good role models for the pupils'.

Annie's passionate belief is that all children can learn and achieve. What she has found particularly satisfying from the start of her teaching career is helping children to improve. She has wanted to work in a school where 'children are fired up with what is being said and done in the classroom'.

That was not her experience of her own education. Apart from two teachers at the grammar school:

> 'I had appalling teachers all the way through and was totally bored from start to finish. I didn't know what the purpose of what we were doing was. I only applied to teacher training college because I couldn't think of what else to do.'

Her experience of teacher training in the east end of London transformed her view of teaching. She saw its potential for changing the lives of children, whatever their background. She enjoyed classroom teaching, always wanting to compare what the children were able to do with what they had been able to do last week and last year:

> 'If I didn't see an improvement, I wanted to know why. What was I doing? Was it right? Could I do it another way?'

As head, Annie has encouraged the staff to ask themselves the same questions, recognising that they are the key to children learning and to the school improving. She has also set about creating an environment where teachers do learn and develop their expertise as highly skilled professionals. This is a continuous process, starting from when the teachers take up their post at the school. One newly qualified teacher spoke of how much she had learned after four weeks. Other teachers had made her feel welcome and provided practical help and advice, whether it was un-jamming the photocopier, handling a difficult child or helping a child cope with bereavement. She had also received valuable advice and support from her mentor, who was the leader of her year team. As well as informal contact, they met once a week for 30 minutes to discuss how things were going. This had been particularly helpful in giving her practical ideas for making target-setting work relevant for individual children in her class.

The head had also helped her, dealing in her company with a child whose behaviour was causing her problems in class. Annie had followed up an incident at dinnertime when the child was alleged to have hit another pupil. The head had:

◆ given the child a fair hearing;
◆ found out exactly what had happened;
◆ ensured that the girl responsible had apologised and that both girls had made it up;

◆ used the incident to explore with the child her patterns of behaviour;

◆ gone through with her the consequences of that behaviour;

◆ worked out with her ways of behaving appropriately in future.

The intervention was highly effective: the girl's behaviour in class improved dramatically, which removed the teacher's main source of anxiety. Annie had also shown the teacher how to deal with similar situations in the future. The teacher observed that the head had been both fair and firm; despite the child's agitated interruptions early on, the head had kept calm and not raised her voice. Above all, she had shown the child an alternative way of behaving and expressed a belief in her that she would make the necessary change.

Other teachers commented on the level of support provided by the head in dealing with difficult situations. One teacher compared this school with her previous school where the head was conciliatory and weak in the face of aggressive parents:

> 'They were allowed to come in and shout at you and nothing was ever done. Here we never have to see a parent by ourselves if we feel we need support. And Annie will tell an aggressive parent that they will have to come back later if they can't calm down.'

Issues of concern raised by parents are normally dealt with straightaway in a calm and constructive atmosphere involving all concerned, including the child.

Another teacher had returned to the school after gaining promotion elsewhere. She had felt unhappy in her new school because 'any ideas I had were literally shouted down by the head'. She described the ethos of Bridge Market as one where 'people listen to you, value your ideas and share problems'. Teachers sort out problems at their level, knowing that the head and deputy will intervene and provide support if they are needed:

> 'I have exactly the same challenges in this school as in my last school. Here I see them as positive, like when children are misbehaving you see that as "Right how can I tackle that behaviour?" When you are not happy, as I wasn't in my previous school, you see the same challenge as negative. It wears you down and you think you are not a very good teacher.'

The head and the deputy work together to create an environment where teachers do feel confident about their professional competence and want to improve. Teachers receive systematic feedback through appraisal, which includes classroom observation. The deputy is one of the appraisers. She has a good overall view of the qualities of the teachers:

◆ as a result of her work as special educational needs co-ordinator (SENCO);
◆ through taking each teacher's class one day a term during their release time for subject development work.

She described her approach:

> 'In appraisal, I always look for the good things. I tend to go into lessons and think that's a good idea, I must try that. And then I pick up on issues that need building on.'

Following appraisal, Annie has a separate interview with each teacher, looking at their long-term professional development and career ambition. In the light of the appraisal and career interview, the head and deputy work with teachers on developing skills in need of attention, such as people management or active listening. One teacher remarked of the deputy:

> 'She will always drag out the best from any situation and give you a positive point to start on. Something I have learned massively from her is the power of listening to a child and acknowledging that you have heard them.'

Annie attaches a great deal of importance to teachers gaining good subject knowledge in all areas of the curriculum. Their job is, in her words, 'to provide a diet of meat and potatoes, not slop'. Each teacher, other than the NQTs, is responsible for a subject area. They are given one day per term to use for subject development, which they may decide to use:

◆ to audit or organise resources;
◆ to sample children's work;
◆ to observe teachers teach their subject;
◆ to provide classroom help and guidance through team teaching;
◆ to visit exhibitions;
◆ to attend training.

Each teacher is expected to lead a staff workshop at least once a year, bringing colleagues up to date on developments in their subject. This approach enables each teacher to develop a subject expertise; it shares the load evenly amongst the teaching staff and is an effective way of ensuring that everyone is sufficiently knowledgeable in all areas of the curriculum. Opportunities are provided for teachers to observe colleagues teach particular subjects or topics in areas of the curriculum where they feel less confident.

Annie also acts as an informed, vigilant and active gatekeeper, interpreting, modifying and sometimes challenging the government agenda. Her criteria are simple: Does what is required help teachers to do their job better, adding value to what they do? Bureaucracy is kept to the minimum and teachers are urged to do only the planning and paperwork needed for them to do their job well and for the head and the deputy to have an overall view of what is happening in each classroom. The literacy hour was substantially modified after the head realised that it was having some very negative effects:

◆ deskilling teachers;
◆ turning children off literature;
◆ rendering children less capable of extended writing.

Returning from an acting headship in another school, Annie realised that all was not well with the literacy hour after listening to teachers' concerns, looking at their lesson plans and observing literacy lessons. She concluded that highly skilled teachers, some of whom 'will set a class alight with their love of literature', were losing confidence in their own professional judgement as they sought to do everything that was required of them in the highly structured literacy hour. Following a staff workshop led by the literacy co-ordinator, plus an in-service session run by an outside expert, it was decided to restrict the literacy hour to three sessions a week, using the other days to do extended writing and read literature. Again, this is an example of a school harnessing government initiatives to its own needs rather than putting on a prescribed straitjacket.

Annie – with excellent support from key stakeholders including the deputy and the chair of governors – has succeeded in transforming the culture of the school. The social and academic profile of the children is more mixed than it was when she took over, but their standards of attainment are higher. To achieve this she has used a range of leadership styles:

◆ She makes extensive use of the **authoritative style**, transmitting her own strongly held beliefs into a clear vision of what the school stands for, which is shared and acted on enthusiastically by the staff.

◆ In the first two years she used the **coercive style** to deal with unacceptable behaviour from some members of staff.

◆ This has been replaced increasingly by the **affiliative style**, which she and the deputy use to create a warm collegial atmosphere where people help each other, see the funny side of things and recognise that everyone is human.

◆ She uses the **democratic style** in staff discussions about curriculum issues and when seeking views on ways of moving the school forward. There are limits to the use of this style if the majority view conflicts with her own fundamental beliefs and values. This was evident in the decision over whether to set children for maths. According to one teacher:

> 'We had a big debate about setting in maths. Everyone was able to air their views and most were in favour of it, even though we knew Annie wouldn't agree to it. She presented her evidence to show that setting was a self-fulfilling prophecy. Children in Set 3 would behave like children in Set 3, and Set 3 teachers would behave like Set 3 teachers and lose their confidence to teach at a higher level. We felt we would be able to discuss it again after we had done the training for the numeracy hour, but since then it hasn't come up as an issue.'

◆ Both the head and deputy make extensive use of the **coaching style**. They do this by:

◆ role modelling desired behaviour;
◆ providing specific feedback on teachers' skills and attributes;
◆ discussing with staff their long-term goals;
◆ generally promoting a culture that encourages self-improvement.

Changing school culture: Orchard School

'When things are steep, remember to stay level-headed.' — Horace

Orchard School is an 11–19 comprehensive school with 1,500 pupils. The main school is girls only; the sixth form is mixed. The school is situated in a deprived urban area. Forty-one per cent of the pupils are eligible for free school meals; 37% speak English as an additional language; 47% are from minority ethnic groups; 30% have special educational needs.

Hannah Marchant took over as head six years ago. The school had a falling roll and a poor reputation in the local area. Today, the school is oversubscribed. The examination results for 2000 show a marked improvement, most probably reflecting both a slightly more balanced intake and an improvement in the organisation and climate. Thirty-seven per cent of the pupils gained five or more grades A–C, compared with 19% in 1993; 91% gained five or more grades A–G, compared with 78% in 1993; and 100% achieved one or more grades from A–G, compared with 87% in 1993. The 1999 OFSTED report concluded that 'the pupils achieved higher standards of attainment than would be expected in similar schools'. It continued:

'Both the headteacher and the governing body provide very strong leadership and a clear and effective educational direction for the school. The headteacher . . . is well supported by an able, cohesive and well-balanced management team, which in turn is generally well supported at middle management level . . . staff at all levels in the school are firmly committed to giving pupils the best quality of education that they can achieve.'

Hannah began the headship determined to transform Orchard School into a high-achieving school for all the pupils and a school to which everyone felt proud to belong. She was brought up within a mixed-race family living on a council estate in Edinburgh. She was the first member of her family to go to university:

'If it hadn't been for committed parents, the welfare state and a good education, I wouldn't have been able to achieve what I have been able to achieve. It was one of my teachers, "Granny" Wilson, who said to me, "Why aren't you applying to university?" I said that I hadn't thought about it. She said that I should go on and teach because "you would be good at it". I followed her advice, did a degree and went on to teacher training college. I see it as my job to make sure that every child has the same chances that I've had. I am really committed to that.'

After her appointment, and before she started as head, Hannah spoke to a number of key people in the school about what they saw its strengths and weaknesses to be and what areas needed development. From these discussions and her own observations immediately after she took up post, she came to the conclusion that the main problem facing the school was that, despite the presence of a number of committed staff, the predominant cultural attitude was that the school was there for the staff and not the pupils. Another related problem was that the support staff didn't feel part of the school, and the administrative structure was extremely inefficient. For example, accurate financial information was hard to come by and it was difficult to get papers produced for governors' meetings.

At her first meeting for all staff Hannah talked about her vision for the school, what she expected from the staff and what she expected from the students. She emphasised that Orchard School was there for all to achieve in the widest sense, and that it would be a school were everyone was valued. At a subsequent meeting staff revised and crystallised the aims of the school and from this the pupils were asked to think of an appropriate motto. They came up with 'Success and Harmony', which is continually referred to in order to remind everyone of what the school stands for. She then set about identifying what this meant for individuals, clarifying what each person was responsible for, to whom they were accountable and what systems and processes everyone needed to carry out. She used an external consultant to review existing organisational structures, as a result of which she entirely reorganised the support services and built clearly defined line-management responsibilities into the brief of the senior management team. She established a statement of operating procedures to achieve consistency of approach in all areas of school organisation.

Hannah also set up a formal consultation process, inviting all staff to contribute their views on any proposed changes, and she introduced a daily morning briefing meeting for all staff. This, in her view, has played an important part in shifting the culture and creating a sense of community and common purpose. Before the briefing she meets with the deputies to decide on the content. The briefing always begins with something positive that has taken place, and the member of staff responsible is thanked. The briefing goes on to inform staff of events and to highlight any area that needs staff attention, such as homework or uniform.

In the words of one member of staff, 'for Hannah, second best is not good enough'. That goes for everything: how the buildings are looked after, the school prospectus, letters going home, the quality of teaching, how pupils behave both in and out of school. Hannah and the members of the senior management team maintain an active presence around the school. One teacher said: 'Hannah is always coming down the corridor.' She finds out what is going on, picks up areas that need attention, praises and encourages where due, provides support where necessary and challenges people where behaviour is at variance with school values and procedures. Early on in her headship she started disciplinary proceedings against the senior administrative officer, who was providing a very inefficient service and undermining her authority. He subsequently left. She reprimanded a staff governor who had issued confidential budget papers to all staff and who later had been abusive towards a colleague in the staff room. More recently, she started competency proceedings against two members of staff whose teaching was not up to the required standard, but only after the senior deputy had provided an extensive programme of support that had not led to sufficient improvement. On another occasion she followed the school's sickness and absence policy to deal with the long-term absence of a middle manager, which led to his dismissal. Hannah also stuck to her guns in the early stages of her headship when pushing through unpopular measures designed to avoid a budget deficit.

What Hannah has done in the six years of her headship is to secure the commitment of the staff who are willing 'to go the extra mile'. This is evident from the extensive programme of extra-curricular activities, the care and attention given to lesson preparation and the views of the staff we interviewed. A key reason for this is that she has articulated values shared by staff about the importance of what they are doing to make a difference to the lives of young people growing up in a multi-racial community marked by widespread poverty and deprivation. A teacher who recently left the school for promotion said in her farewell speech that if we achieve here, as we are, with all the different races and cultures getting to know each other and getting on with each other, then there is hope for the world.

Crucially, staff have seen that during Hannah's headship their efforts, both individually and collectively, are making a difference. Shortly after she arrived she told staff that the most pressing priority was both to increase pupil numbers and to achieve a more balanced comprehensive intake. This involved everyone, teachers and support staff, in improving the quality of what they were providing and publicising their achievements within the local community and the neighbouring primary schools. The head and the senior management team provided visible and effective support for staff by managing discipline in the corridors and using temporary exclusions as a tool for improving poor behaviour. They also encouraged the pupils to feel that the school was for them – through assemblies, reward systems and having form captains meeting once a week with the head with an open agenda for discussion. Immediate improvements within the school were accompanied by an increase in pupil numbers and a slight shift towards a more balanced intake. The improvements have continued. One teacher commented:

> 'This is a good place to work. It is demanding, but you do feel it is going somewhere. In the three years that I have been at the school, I have seen real progress with students' work as well as their behaviour in the corridors. We have a ridiculous amount of work to do with the government changing Key Stage 3 and the post-16 syllabuses at the same time, but what you cling on to is that we are working in a school where things are improving and we are all committed to its improvement.'

While Hannah is insistent on staff following procedures, she encourages them to use their initiative and try out new ideas, backing them wherever possible:

> 'If anyone has a proposal, I like them to go ahead and try it and I will give them the support to do it. It is only by experimenting and moving things on that the school can develop and the staff can develop.'

The head of music has been at the school for sixteen years and has built up an excellent department with innovative and imaginative teaching. Music tuition remains free, with fourteen instrumental tutors teaching 250 students. There is a school street band, a music club, a senior choir, steel pans, a sitar group and ensembles, all of which perform in school concerts and at various community events. The school has recently become a specialist performing arts college. The head of music commented:

> 'It is only because of Hannah's commitment that we have still got free music tuition. She has found the extra money for it. She was also the driving force behind our successful bid to become a performing arts college. The day after the OFSTED inspectors left she said to us, "Right, let's get started on the bid." She is really out for what the kids can achieve. She wants the best for them and in

her heart of hearts she feels that. She has always provided support and makes me feel like I'm doing a good job. She listens to me and makes me feel like I'm valued. I know heads of music in other schools who are just as good as I am but who have given up because they haven't had the support.'

Hannah has created a highly effective senior management team that transmits with one voice the culture of high expectations, support and praise. She made it clear from the start that she wanted them to express their views freely within their meetings, but that once they had decided the common line on a particular issue, it was everybody's line. One member of the senior management team observed:

'You have got to have a team that works well. You have to have a team that is seen by the staff as working with the same sort of principles, getting on well with each other and working as a team. In our senior management meetings there is a lot to discuss and do. The tone is open and there is quite a lot of humour and banter (we tease Hannah about what she sees as her lack of counselling skills) but everyone is very clear that the work is done and done to a high standard.'

One member of staff in her second year of teaching said the senior management team was:

'very supportive and warm. I feel that I can trust them and tell them when I am having a difficulty and when I am having a success. It might be just a chat over the photocopier.'

The example of the head and the senior management team influences the way middle managers lead and motivate their staff. An inexperienced teacher referred to one head of year (HoY) who came up to her and said that one of the girls in her year was telling her how much she was enjoying *Macbeth* in her lesson. The teacher went on to say:

'other teachers boosting each other's morale is really important because teaching is a lonely job and you have low days'.

For her, the ethos and working practices of the department, reflecting the core values of the school, provided an invaluable source of guidance and mutual support:

'The department is based on people working together. We have equal roles. We are expected to work very hard and contribute to resources. When you've done that it is welcomed.'

This teacher had received vital support from Hannah at a critical time, during an OFSTED inspection that occurred in her fifth week of teaching. The inspector, who had observed part of her lesson, afterwards told her that her provision for bilingual pupils and her lesson planning was excellent, but her lesson was unsatisfactory because the pupils had not moved from a state of not knowing to a state of knowing about the particular leaflet they were studying. The teacher said:

'On the following day I was walking into school at the same time as the head. She saw that I was crying. She took me into her office, listened and talked to me for about half an hour and just calmed me down. She then relayed her concerns to the Registered Inspector about what had happened. Following that, I was observed teaching another lesson which was judged to be "good".'

Since then the head has observed her teach two lessons, praised the quality of her teaching, given her helpful advice on the value and use of humour in the classroom and encouraged her to create time to pursue other interests outside school.

Hannah has succeeded in transforming the culture of the school to one where the pupils come first. She and the senior management team have used a wide range of leadership styles to bring this about. She herself uses the **coercive** and **pace-setting styles** in the continuing drive to raise standards. She uses the **authoritative style** to create a compelling picture of the school's journey to a better future. As one of the deputies commented:

'Hannah has a long-term vision. Everyone knows what she wants for the school. She says it very clearly. She is also very good at praising people for what they are contributing to the school. She does this publicly at the morning briefing meeting and privately through a note or thank-you card.'

As the incident with the distraught teacher demonstrated, she also uses the **affiliative style** where appropriate. Through the consultation procedure, the senior management team makes use of the **democratic**

style, although there is the perception amongst some staff that on particular issues, such as the format of reports, the decision has already been taken. Her senior deputy, who is responsible for staff development, is particularly skilled in the use of the **coaching style**. She makes good use of this in helping teachers develop their classroom expertise. One of the strengths of the senior managers is their recognition and use of complementary skills, qualities and styles across the team.

Summary

Anonymous

> 'It is alright to be looking for compliments – to give to somebody else.'

◆ Leadership in action requires certain management skills but is not defined, nor adequately described, in terms of these skills alone.

◆ Effective leadership requires continual adaptation to circumstantial and environmental factors.

◆ The tenacity to believe in oneself and the sought after mission, in the face of professional resistance and possibly personal defamation, is the cornerstone of applied leadership.

Field Marshal Montgomery

> 'Leadership can be the loneliest job in the world.'

◆ Effective leadership includes moving easily from one role to another, and from one approach to alternative approaches.

◆ Leaders inspire confidence in others, otherwise the venture fails.

◆ Though leaders inspire, motivate and model, they do not win by unique individualism alone. Effective leadership results in better team work.

Overview

In this chapter we move from the particular to the general. We do this to find answers to the question: What is it that the headteachers have done to motivate their staff and get the best out of them. In the following analysis there is no attempt to erect a grand theory or model. We are very aware that the sample of schools is small; that there are important differences relating to size and phase of school; that there are important contextual variations; and that in all of these situations there is no one way to achieve excellence. However, we did find that, despite these subtle differences, there were certain common elements in how the heads approached their leadership task and in what they did. These elements are of relevance beyond the case study contexts and they have meaning for all school leaders and for those concerned with school improvement:

◆ All the heads passionately believed in the importance of what they were doing – enabling themselves and their staff to transform children's lives.
◆ They converted their beliefs into convincing and compelling visions that secured the commitment of their staff.
◆ They made effective use of different leadership styles to create the organisational climate where staff gave of their best and therefore moved the school closer towards its vision.
◆ In selecting the appropriate style and using it effectively, the heads drew on high levels of spiritual, cognitive and emotional levels of intelligence.
◆ By exercising intelligent leadership, the heads enabled staff to preserve and strengthen their educational values and vision and meet the requirements of the government reform programme.

In this chapter, we look at these elements in turn.

Passionate belief

'The distance doesn't matter; it is only the first step that is difficult.'

Marquise Du
Deffand

All the heads had a passionate belief in the importance of what they were doing. They shared the conviction that education has the potential to transform the lives of everyone, regardless of class, ethnicity or gender. Most were drawn to the challenge of making a difference to the lives of disadvantaged groups and individuals. The formulation of the mission varied according to the head's own beliefs and experiences:

◆ 'bringing people to life . . . enabling them to become more fully human and thus closer to God';
◆ 'making students feel good about themselves so that they feel able to go into the world and make a difference';
◆ 'enabling students to realise they had important choices to make which would profoundly affect their own lives';
◆ opening up students' minds to the richness of life and its possibilities by 'firing their imagination and curiosity'.

These beliefs are based on an optimistic view of human nature. The stance is that everyone has the potential to learn, develop, achieve and enrich their own lives and those of others. There is respect for each individual as a human being, as well as appreciation of individual uniqueness and potential. What the heads are not prepared to tolerate is a member of staff using their authority in a manner that demonstrates disrespect for others – sarcasm, bullying or loss of self-control.

The heads know from their own experience the power of education to transform. They also know from experience how children in schools and classrooms are too often bored by teaching that closes rather than opens their minds. They appreciate how easy it is to lower self-esteem, not raise it; to reinforce rather than challenge the status quo; to practise the familiar as opposed to seeking new horizons. They are acutely aware that if education is to be exciting and meaningful, the teachers are the agents of transformation who will make it happen. Good teaching:

◆ brings 'children to life';
◆ enables them to feel good about themselves;
◆ encourages them to observe and question;
◆ provides them with an appetite for learning that stays in place for life.

Headteachers can, and in our case study examples often did, provide inspirational, thought-provoking assemblies, and they also taught model lessons (although time pressures made this exceptional). Importantly, they recognised that the impact of their messages and modelling is limited unless teachers provide similar signals and learning experiences day in and day out. In general, what these heads have done is use their authority and influence to create a school culture and organisational climate that enables and encourages all staff to act as 'change agents' (see pp. 165–6). Their approach is clear because they know:

◆ what qualities and characteristics they want the students in their charge to develop;
◆ that these attributes will take root only if the staff feel good about themselves and the work they are doing;
◆ that the required commitment develops only when staff can ask questions and contribute to decisions in an open climate;
◆ that the staff themselves need to be learners, continually reflecting on their experiences and skills;
◆ that the staff will treat students appropriately if they receive respect and understanding from their managers.

Strategic PIN down – Reflection 4.1	**Aim**	
	◆ to consider your own beliefs and personal values.	
	P – State the PROBLEM	Because of pressures of work and the emphasis in western culture on doing many things at once, we frequently do not create time to . . .
	I – Clarify the ISSUE	To make it a priority to consider what we regard of fundamental importance – what gives our lives purpose – we . . .
	N – Tackle the NEED	In order to convey our passionate beliefs and personal values to others, we must show in our behaviour and actions . . .

Before you begin, imagine, as in the exercise proposed by Talbot (2000), that:

'You are on your death bed, life ebbing away. Reflect on the things that have made your life worthwhile and the things you regret. What does this tell you about the things that you value for their own sake?'

p. 18

Tip

Think about the course of your own career and what you have achieved. To what extent do the achievements reflect and help to explain your fundamental beliefs?

Convincing and compelling visions

Lincoln Steffens

> 'I have seen the future and it works!'

All the case study heads succeeded in converting their passionate beliefs into a convincing and compelling vision of what the school **could** and **would** become. This picture of the future won over the hearts and minds of most staff. It secured their commitment. It became the force to move thinking and actions.

Values in common

First, the vision accorded with their fundamental professional beliefs and values. As Barth (1990) has pointed out:

> 'All of us begin our work in education with a 20/20 personal vision about the way we like our school to be. This is what we value and are prepared to work for and even fight for. That is why we became educators . . . [but then our] capacity to retain and adhere to a personal vision becomes blunted by exhaustion and compliance . . . so our visions take refuge way down in our hip-pockets where, in too many cases, they forever languish rather than inspire.'

p. 148

Barth goes on to argue that the principal task of the educational leader is to extract these visions from the hip-pockets so that they again contribute to the collective vision and re-energise each individual, since:

p. 151

> 'Vision unlocked is energy unlocked.'

Our heads unlocked vision in different ways. The head of Forest Oak interviewed teachers and asked them what they wanted the school to become. The head of Ridgeway asked staff and governors to consider in groups the question. 'What are we here for?' Others provided staff with an opportunity to reflect on purpose within the context of practical discussions on curriculum issues, such as the literacy hour or the best way to provide for very able students. Whatever the approach, the staff we interviewed were explicit about what their school stood for and they believed in the importance of what they were doing. In particular, they were clear about how their specific roles related to the bigger picture.

Authenticity

Second, the staff saw that the heads genuinely held to their vision. It was not presentation rhetoric or a temporal fad. It motivated the heads, and they were seen to act in accordance with their stated values and beliefs. They demonstrated respect for the uniqueness of the individual. They recognised each person had a significant contribution to make. They asked individuals for their thoughts and feelings on particular issues. They involved them in seeking solutions to real problems – such as when the head of Stow Cross asked the lunchtime supervisor whether she thought children should be called to lunch instead of having to queue.

Credibility

Third, the vision and major goals were realistic. They could be achieved. Their essence was modelled on a day-to-day basis by the heads, who showed individuals what they needed to do and how they needed to behave to realise the vision in practice. For example, by working alongside the newly qualified teacher, the head of Bridge Market showed her how to deal with difficult situations in the future and, through her example, the head gave this teacher ideas about how she might act to prevent such situations from recurring.

The heads also dealt effectively with obstacles in the way of securing the vision. They demonstrated a hard-edged determination to achieve the best for their students, regardless of difficulties. Critically, this included tackling staff who were not prepared to play their part in moving themselves and the school forward. In five of the six schools, the heads took painful but highly visible and decisive action. This resulted in some staff departing. In the final analysis the message was clear: you either sign up or ship out.

Common to all six schools was that by one means or another, including very careful attention to the process of selecting new staff, the heads acquired a critical mass of colleagues who were committed to going the extra mile in order to do their best for students and to secure shared educational goals.

In all the schools the heads forged effective relationships with senior teachers and other team leaders, and they made use of the expertise of these key members of staff by encouraging them to play the role of coach, enforcer, referee, entrepreneur or whatever role was required by the issue of the moment. At Forest Oak, for example, the coaching skills of the deputy complemented the vision-building and systems-maintenance skills of the head. In general, the heads used senior or experienced colleagues as:

◆ prime sources of information about what was happening in the school;
◆ a sounding board and source of ideas about what needed to happen;
◆ the principal agents, particularly in the larger schools, for making sure change did happen.

Systems support

Fourth, the heads in our study set up effective systems and processes to make the vision achievable. In particular, they examined ways to enable teachers to do their job better. Improvements secured included:

◆ clear policies on managing behaviour in positive ways;
◆ streamlined approaches to lesson planning, so that staff could work more easily together and share responsibility for lesson outcomes;
◆ the creation of some non-contact time in the primary schools to help staff develop their subject knowledge and broaden professional expertise;
◆ lesson observation, careers interviews and staff development activities to support programmes of self-improvement.

In addition, all the heads had in place effective systems for gathering information, ensuring that policies and procedures were being applied and identifying areas for priority attention. The systems included formal monitoring, such as that on marking at Ridgeway, or informal data gathering, as demonstrated at Bridge Market, where the head was first alerted to problems in the structure of the literacy hour after listening to teachers in the staff room. The head of Orchard School used the morning briefing meetings to point out to staff those areas that needed everyone's attention, thereby reinforcing the principle that consistency in approach makes professional life easier.

What was striking about the staff we interviewed was that they didn't view accountability as a chore or threat. The way it had been explained and introduced reinforced the opportunity provided by accountability procedures for staff to explain to others what they were doing and what they had achieved.

Emotional support

Fifth, the heads applied these systems and processes in ways that encouraged staff to feel good about themselves; to recognise their value to the school; to feel they could share problems with the wider community; and to feel their ideas and humour helped cement collegial thinking and actions. In particular, we noted that heads and members of the leadership groups made significant interventions when they interacted swiftly and positively with individual members of staff at important moments for them. They did so by giving advice, providing support, recognising positive work and appreciating specific pieces of endeavour. The net effect was to sustain positive professionalism. Such interventions included:

◆ helping teachers to deal with difficult students or parents;
◆ reminding staff of their professional attributes and worth (for example, support to the teacher reduced to tears after critical comments from an inspector);
◆ providing emotional and practical support at a time of personal bereavement;
◆ thanking colleagues for high-quality work or extra effort;
◆ giving clear and constructive feedback after lesson observation.

All the heads paid particular attention to the manner and means of giving feedback on lessons and other observed work. The approach was to ensure that feedback enhanced self-awareness about qualities as teachers, gave practical ideas for improving practice, provided clear targets for professional development and, whenever possible, contributed to staff feeling good about themselves both individually and collectively. Progress towards key developments was reported regularly, so that individuals and teams could see what they were contributing to the school as a whole.

In some instances a head decided that individual teachers were experiencing difficulties that had wider ramifications. This was the case at Walpole with regard to the delivery of the literacy hour and provision for very able students. The response was to explore the issue collectively in a series of workshops or through the use of in-service education and training (INSET) time. This encouraged a collaborative problem-solving approach to the issue, while reducing any feeling that the climate was one in which teachers had to struggle on their own.

Leadership styles and organisational climate

Abraham Lincoln

'Determine that the thing can and shall be done, and then we shall find the way.'

In motivating staff to give of their best in pursuit of the shared vision, these successful heads made effective use of a wide range of leadership styles. The use of different styles had a positive effect on each school's culture and organisational climate, generally making it a more harmonious place to work and contributing significantly to its enhanced performance.

All used the **authoritative style** to establish **clarity** about vision and values and what each person's **responsibility** was in realising these. The declaration of the vision and values varied somewhat – a mission statement, a list of core values or a general statement of purpose. However, there was common base, as each statement:

◆ encapsulated the core beliefs held by the head and staff;
◆ included reference to all staff, not just teachers;
◆ was used by the head as a powerful instrument to move the school away from the actual and closer to the ideal.

At Forest Oak, different aspects of the mission statement were reviewed every year by staff and pupils. At Ridgeway, the statement at the entrance, 'Beyond this point, learning is the most important thing we do', was used to explore, through staff workshops, ways in which teachers could enrich and accelerate learning.

The **authoritative style** was used to promote confidence and **flexibility**. Ideas were requested from various audiences; policies and procedures were repeatedly explained so that they helped rather than hindered teacher effectiveness; and, as in the case of the literacy hour, authority was more directly aligned with pedagogy, thereby giving teachers confidence in their own judgements rather than expecting them merely to conform to the rule book. The **authoritative style** was also used to establish understanding that high **standards** were non-negotiable: striving to achieve challenging targets was expected of everyone.

Use was made of the **coercive style** when individual or collective **standards** were low in areas of professional performance and behaviour. A few of the heads made use of the **pace-setting style** when urgent tasks required completion, such as getting ready for an OFSTED inspection towards the start of their headship. All made use of the **coaching style** as a key device for raising **standards**. Five of the six schools had set up formal systems of classroom observation, which they were using to provide teachers with constructive feedback. Staff also had the opportunity to develop their skills and knowledge through courses, visits to other schools or observing other teachers teach. All of the heads went out of their way to ensure that intrinsic and extrinsic **rewards** were in place. At the very least, good performance and additional effort were acknowledged and valued, and, where possible, these qualities received recognition through promotion.

The heads used varying degrees of the **democratic** and **affiliative styles** primarily to foster **team commitment**, although some used the **democratic style** to provide **clarity** and knowledge about the best way forward. At Ridgeway, for example, the head asked staff and governors to choose one of the three OFSTED issues for action, then to share their knowledge in groups through brainstorming and so to reach possible solutions.

Overall, the use of the **democratic style** depended on the beliefs of the head and the educational context in which they were operating. At Forest Oak, the head used the style infrequently because she was concerned that democratic decision-making might lead to poor decisions. At Bridge Market, where the head used a broadly consultative approach, she was not prepared to move to setting, despite it being the preference of most staff, because it conflicted with her basic beliefs and the evidence she had gathered from research and her own experience. At Stow Cross, part of the head's basic value system was a belief that everyone should have a say in decisions that affected them. When teachers made it clear they were not in favour of her proposal to replace one literacy hour with work on creative thinking, she dropped the idea.

The three primary heads made extensive use of the **affiliative style**, as they came into frequent, informal contact with individual members of staff. They saw maintaining friendly relations and demonstrating a genuine interest in each individual as being necessary to secure **team commitment**, as well as being important in its own right. In the larger secondary schools the **affiliative style** was used when the head was comfortable using it and felt it appropriate for a task or communication in hand.

All of the heads made extensive use of two of the styles associated with long-term performance, the **authoritative** and **coaching styles**. They made sure that everyone knew what the school stood for, how important that was, and what everyone needed to do to achieve the principal goals. They also gave constructive feedback to individuals on how they were doing, using this to recognise and value each person's contribution while providing advice on how to make that contribution even more significant. Most used the **democratic** and **affiliative styles** to develop a **collaborative** climate, and they used the **coercive** and **pace-setting styles** as situations determined. Everyone used the **coercive style** to challenge and rectify any stakeholder behaviour that undermined the core beliefs and mission.

Why were the heads able to use these styles so effectively? It is not a question of each one being set off when triggered by a particular situation. They used their judgement as to what style was appropriate for a particular situation, often changing styles frequently within a short period of time. They also had to combine the styles effectively to achieve the overall purpose. To understand the approach that is needed precisely when it is needed is the essence of applied management. It requires strong insights into how and why people act as they do, coupled with appreciating what each person can and does contribute to the development plan and to the school as a whole.

Different intelligences

Anonymous

> 'It's not enough to be smart – one must know **when** to be smart.'

To answer the question, Why were the heads able to use these different styles effectively?, we need to relate our observations to recent thinking about the nature of intelligence. We suggest that the heads were able to use their leadership styles effectively, to motivate and to manage their staff, because they could apply high levels of three different intelligences – spiritual, cognitive and emotional.

Spiritual intelligence

Spiritual intelligence has been defined by Zohar and Marshall (2000) as:

> 'The intelligence with which we address and solve problems of meaning and value, the intelligence with which we can place our actions and our lives in a wider, richer, meaning giving context, the intelligence with which we can assess that one course of action or life-path is more meaningful than another.'

p. 3

As humans we are driven to ask fundamental questions about meaning and purpose in our lives. We long to give our lives, ourselves and our behaviour a sense of worth and meaning. We are, as Stephen Gould (1991) argues:

> 'pattern-seeking animals. We must find cause and meaning in all events.'

p. 60

The case study heads had a strong set of personal values that derived from either religious or secular experiences. It is their passionate attachment to these values that invests their work as heads with special significance and meaning. They use these values, also held by their colleagues, to steer the direction of the school and to underpin its work with collective endeavour and shared purpose.

Cognitive intelligence

Evidence from all the case studies suggests that the heads were, at the very least, demonstrating what Goleman (2000) calls 'threshold capabilities' or 'entry level requirements' for the position of headship in the area of cognitive intelligence. By cognitive intelligence, we mean the ability to reason and conceptualise: in particular, the ability to formulate and test hypotheses; to gather evidence, analyse data and see patterns and connections; to devise logical solutions to problems and work out sequential action plans.

The case study heads were deploying this intelligence to engage in strategic thinking, which includes taking into account the present context as well as anticipated local, national and global trends. It was also in continual use at the micro level as heads evaluated lessons, analysed trends in results of SATs, identified the essential elements that needed to go into the school's behaviour policy, or skimmed the latest government circular to work out an appropriate response. And, of course, the heads used their cognitive intelligence to set up systems and action plans designed to move the school forward.

Emotional intelligence

But, by themselves, systems and action plans are of limited use. What matters is whether people use them, how they use them and to what purpose and effect. This depends to a large extent on collective commitment. Staff we interviewed were committed to what they were doing, and they used the school's strategic planning and systems to do their job well. What the heads did was to steer that commitment. In achieving this they demonstrated high levels of emotional intelligence. Goleman (1998a) sees this intelligence as:

> 'the capacity for recognising our own feelings and those of others, for motivating ourselves, and for managing emotions well in ourselves and in our relationships. It describes abilities distinct from, but complementary to, academic intelligence, the purely cognitive capacities measured by IQ.'

p. 317

Different levels of emotional intelligence

According to Glass (1996), emotional intelligence can be seen as having three levels (see Figure 2):

Mastery of the inner self deals with our ability to understand our own emotions, to manage them and to motivate ourselves.

Perception of others addresses our capacity to understand other people's emotions and to empathise with them.

Interaction with others considers our social skills – how successfully we interest, motivate and lead others.

p. 16

We have seen that in the case study schools the heads were very effective at the third level – interaction with others. They showed a high degree of social skill in 'moving people in the direction they desire' (Goleman 1998b). This is a critical skill for contemporary heads who have to persuade often stressed and sceptical staff to adjust to externally driven change that is designed to alter their way of working. The heads demonstrated the capacity to communicate effectively with different audiences for different purposes and to manage relationships with others, including team-building and the resolution of conflict.

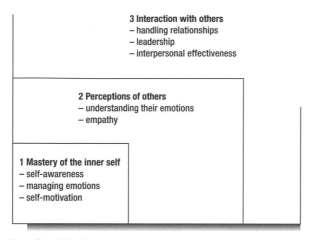

Figure 2: The three levels of emotional intelligence

3 Interaction with others
– handling relationships
– leadership
– interpersonal effectiveness

2 Perceptions of others
– understanding their emotions
– empathy

1 Mastery of the inner self
– self-awareness
– managing emotions
– self-motivation

Source: Glass 1996, p. 16

Goleman's research makes clear that success at the third level – interaction with others – depends on our degree of emotional intelligence at the first two levels. Emotional intelligence at all levels is rooted in our own self-awareness: understanding our inner drives, having an accurate perception of our strengths and weaknesses and using that understanding to manage our own behaviour. Emotionally intelligent people keep disruptive feelings under control, ensure that they behave with integrity in a way that is consistent with their values and maintain high levels of motivation to achieve.

Understanding oneself is a prerequisite for understanding others. At the second level, emotional intelligence involves the capacity to empathise with others, to see where they are coming from and to understand what is driving their behaviour. It also extends to an awareness of what makes an organisation tick in terms of its culture and centres of influence.

Interesting facts 3   Emotional intelligence, leadership styles and gender

Research suggests that the emotional intelligence of men and women differs in some important respects. What are these differences and what are the implications for school leaders of either sex? It is suggested the differences can be traced back to early childhood. By the age of 3, girls have, on average, twice the vocabulary of boys. They become more skilled at using language to express feelings, minimise conflict and build relationships. Boys, with less facility for language, tend to concentrate on performing tasks and are more at ease in physical and competitive situations. Some evidence from studies of emotional intelligence intimates that these differences carry through into adult life.

Goleman 1998a

◆ An analysis of 1,500 men and women from four continents found identical patterns of strengths and weaknesses for men and women. Women, in general, are more aware of their emotions, show more empathy, are more skilled at interpersonal relationships; in contrast, men present themselves as more self-confident in general and more optimistic. They adapt more easily and handle certain kinds of stress better.

◆ Whilst there are statistically significant differences between men and women in these dimensions of emotional intelligence, there are plenty of exceptions. This means, for example, that some men are more skilled than most women in relating to people; and some women are more capable than most men at dealing with general stress.

◆ Another major study cited by Goleman (1998a) found that men have as much latent ability as women with regard to empathy, but show less of it because it may be interpreted as a sign of weakness – that is, it is not considered to be 'how men should behave'.

◆ The challenges facing contemporary school leaders require them to demonstrate both 'masculine' and 'feminine' characteristics – to be what Bern (1977) describes as 'androgynous' leaders and managers. For example, they need, in some situations, to be able to confront poor performance, not avoid it; while in many other situations they need to be able to 'feel with their colleagues', to take people with them rather than tell them what to do.

◆ In her study of six successful female primary and secondary headteachers Hall (1996) found that they were acting as androgynous leaders: both working collaboratively with colleagues and demonstrating direct authoritative leadership. The five female heads in our case studies were highly effective in their use of the authoritative style, and three out of the five had used the coercive and/or pace-setting styles to drive up standards. Evetts (1994) points out, in her study of twenty secondary headteachers, that there were differences in leadership styles but that few were gender-related. Some of the male heads emphasised collaboration and participative management, while some of the female heads were more directly tough and status-holding in their approach.

◆ What is important is for school leaders to transcend the female/male stereotypes and develop whatever characteristics and styles are necessary to perform their job effectively. They also need to be aware of any gender-based expectations amongst their stakeholders about how they should behave and lead. They may need to prepare a careful response to any stereotypical leanings amongst stakeholders that may hinder their capacity to do the job. For example, the hostility towards Catherine Turner, the head of Stow Cross Primary School on the part of the chair of governors and the 'senior teachers' emanated from perceptions held by these stakeholders about how a young woman head should behave and perform. Also, her values of democracy and collaboration conflicted with theirs. It was impossible to move the school forward until this conflict was resolved.

◆ It is also important for school leaders to appreciate that leadership styles and the notion of different intelligences are 'constructs', not absolutes. They are not universally accepted as accurate or helpful concepts. For example, the reader wishing to see some reservations about the validity of 'multiple intelligences' is referred to White (1998) and Furnham (2000). Neither construct – leadership styles or multiple intelligences – can be applied in an 'off-the-shelf' manner. They serve only as ways to try to understand one's own capabilities and personal reactions, as well as those of the colleagues with whom one shares work.

Case study heads and emotional intelligence

The case study heads showed high degrees of emotional intelligence at the first two of Glass's three levels. At the first level, inner mastery, they drew on their spiritual intelligence to provide them with a strong sense of direction and purpose. They believed in their mission and in their own capacity to see it through. At the same time they welcomed feedback on their own behaviour and performance. The head of Stow Cross, for example, actively sought out feedback and used it to influence her self-perception and the nature of the action she undertook.

All of the heads used self-awareness to manage their own behaviour. The staff perception of the head at Bridge Market was that she remained calm and self-controlled in difficult situations, particularly when other people were angry or upset. All of the heads were also seen by their staff as people of integrity who, since they acted in accordance with strongly held beliefs and took direct personal responsibility to see things through, could be trusted. Finally, at the level of inner self, the heads appeared to use their motivational drive to achieve and to exercise what McClelland (1987) has called 'socialised power' (see pp. 25–6).

The behaviour of the heads included many examples of their capacity to empathise at the levels of the individual, the team and the whole staff. It was empathy with the individual that enabled them to make timely and significant interventions. Empathy with teams and the whole school supported their actions to set up systems of classroom observation that overcame 'institutional suspicion' and won the teachers' belief that the school could move forward.

Emotional intelligence and individual performance

Goleman's research (1998b) led him to conclude that emotional intelligence is the key differentiator of outstanding performance:

> 'When I analysed all this data, I found dramatic results. To be sure, intellect was a driver of outstanding performance. Cognitive skills such as big-picture thinking and long-term vision were particularly important. But when I calculated the ratio of technical skills, IQ and emotional intelligence as ingredients of excellent performance, emotional intelligence proved to be twice as important as others for jobs at all levels.'

p. 94

What is also significant for leadership at all levels and in all types of organisations is that evidence suggests we can develop our emotional intelligence (see Issues in focus 4.1).

Issues in focus 4.1

Emotional intelligence is an indispensable ingredient of effective leadership. To what extent can it be learnt – that is, can one develop one's emotional intelligence? The answer is positive. Emotional intelligence can be refined, provided the individual wants to develop it and is prepared to start by learning more about self.

A good place to begin is to increase one's understanding of the function of the amygdala. This is the oldest part of the brain, designed to cope with survival. Recent neuro-scientific research suggests that as messages enter the brain from our different senses, they go first to the amygdala. Such messages may include sensations that trigger threats to our survival and stir up emotional memories dating back to early childhood. In such a crisis situation, the amygdala takes control of the brain, preventing the message from getting to the thinking part of the brain, the neo-cortex. This process is described by Goleman (1998a) as an 'amygdala hijack'. The hijack may set off behaviour we subsequently regret.

Like other professionals, school leaders are dealing every day with emotionally charged situations that may trigger negative or disruptive feelings in them as well as situations that stimulate positive emotions and make them feel good about themselves and what they are doing. Difficult situations that might trigger a more primitive response could be:

◆ breaking up a fight in the school playground;
◆ dealing with an angry parent complaining about how her child has been treated by a teacher;
◆ challenging poor performance from a member of staff;
◆ being challenged by governors over poor exam results;
◆ receiving a letter from solicitors informing you that a parent is intending to take legal action over alleged bullying.

In the event of an amygdala hijack, the school leader's behaviour in these situations might become aggressive or threatening (perhaps mirroring the behaviour of the other person), defensive and unreasonably yielding, or frozen with everything shut down. Whatever form the behaviour takes, it leads to regret, with the hijacked leader having to deal with the consequences of her/his actions and perhaps thinking 'if only . . .'.

To prevent the hijack from happening, Goleman (1998a) argues that we need to be aware of our emotional triggers. What does make us angry or frightened? What does make us feel happy and fulfilled? Aware of our own emotions, we are in a better position to manage those potentially disruptive emotions in a way that helps us deal with the particular problem we are facing instead of exacerbating it.

Nolan (1987) points to the 'climate for the transaction' and the tendency to adopt the 'adversarial stance' as powerful influences on the way people initially respond to emotional and threatening situations. He believes that politics, the media, films and the corporate identity of some powerful organisations strongly reinforce that a manager or leader's role is to be adversarial in a 'tough' way. Like Goleman, he believes this is counterproductive to good communication and a poor use of the individual's emotional response.

Strategic PIN down – Reflection 4.2	Aim	◆ to develop self-awareness and emotional management.
	P – State the PROBLEM	Our disruptive emotions sometimes affect our behaviour in ways we subsequently . . .
	I – Clarify the ISSUE	In managing our emotions we need to be . . .
	N – Tackle the NEED	To manage our emotions so they . . . our actions, not . . . them.

Before you begin, think about a situation in which you experienced an amygdala hijack.

◆ Why did it have that effect on you? Does it form part of a pattern?

◆ How would you have preferred to behave? Had you done so, how might the outcome have been different?

◆ In the event of a similar situation occurring in the future, how can you prevent an amygdala hijack?

Tip

Get into the habit of a daily activity that enables you to reflect on your feelings. It could be meditation, yoga, going for a walk, keeping a diary, reading a poem, scrutinising a painting or landscape, or listening to a piece of music.

Responding to government reform

Bertrand Russell

'Even when the experts all agree, they may well be mistaken.'

How have the heads in the case studies responded to the demands of the government reform programme? In Chapter 1 we saw that this programme presented school leaders with immense challenges. Schools are now at the centre of political and public debate. They are under more scrutiny now than at any other time in educational history. They face continuous pressure to maintain a cycle of improvement and reach ever higher standards. They are expected to improve outputs of all sorts – levels of attainment, student attendance, student awareness of their role and responsibilities as citizens, parent satisfaction – while lacking control over the key input, the range and nature of the student intake.

The import of business terminology and practice into the educational arena has led to tension and uncertainty amongst teachers over core values and over the key question, What is the primary purpose of the teacher? In general, teachers are more concerned for the development of the whole person and for students to receive a 'rounded' education than they are to secure instrumental goals such as defined percentage increases in specific test results. Tension and uncertainty arise when demands for the latter are seen to obstruct the former. Furthermore, teachers and schools have felt sharply exposed to the seemingly all-powerful gaze of OFSTED, which has taken hold of the classroom key, entering at will to inspect and judge.

The schools in our case studies were successful on three levels:

◆ First, they met the government criteria for success: overall results have improved, standards of attainment have gone up, OFSTED reports have been good, the student roll is buoyant and the schools are seen to be giving good value for money.

◆ Second, each of our case study schools can be said to represent Stoll and Mortimore's (1995) criterion for effectiveness as a school in which:

> 'pupils progress further than might be expected from consideration of its intake'.   p. 1

◆ Third, the schools have moved some way towards realising the visionary aspirations of their leaders. They are places where young minds are 'fired' and young people feel confident about asking questions and making informed choices.

In one of the schools, Forest Oak, the initial success of the new regime led to improvements in the quality of the academic intake, and this has contributed to its sharp upward spiral of improvement. To a lesser extent that is true of Orchard, but not, it appears, of the other schools, where the ability profile has remained more or less the same. Whatever the intake, in terms of quality and overall balance, pupils in these schools have done better than expected.

Our conclusion from the evidence of the case studies is that success on the first two levels was due to success on the third level. What the heads did was to give their staff the confidence to hang onto and, indeed, strengthen their educational values: they did not allow them to 'languish in their hip-pockets' (Barth 1990). Crucially, they also used the external agenda to persuade their staff to modify the traditional teacher-culture of autonomy and make it accessible to constructive influences both from above and from their peers. Thus:

◆ classrooms were opened up to internal observation as an essential preparation for OFSTED;
◆ the national literacy and numeracy strategies were used by the primary heads to promote discussion and share good practice about the teaching of key access skills;
◆ line-management systems were set up in the secondary schools as a vehicle for improving GCSE results and spreading leadership skills into the ranks of the middle managers;
◆ the need to demonstrate consistency enabled the heads to promote stronger whole school approaches to such issues as behaviour management, target setting and planning.

The heads also used quantifiable performance data, within a value-added framework, to set improvement targets and to provide external verification of progress and achievement. Throughout, the heads acted as interpreters and modifiers of the government agenda, not as its compliant mouthpieces. Some government initiatives were delayed or diluted. The literacy programme in all three primary schools was substantially modified in light of the teachers' own experience of what worked best. The instrumental objectives were never seen as the sole, or indeed the main, concern of the teachers' work.

The heads reshaped their school culture in three main ways:

◆ First, they modified existing teacher-culture without attempting to demolish it. Classroom practice was no longer carried out in isolation, but the professional expertise and craft knowledge of the teacher was accorded fundamental respect.
◆ Second, they strengthened hierarchical elements of culture and practice to provide quality assurance and accountability. Through line-management arrangements and systematic monitoring of all areas, the heads had a clear view of how good the school was and where and what action was needed to improve it.
◆ Third, they strengthened the collaborative dimension through the use of coaching, collective problem-solving and the sharing of good practice and planning.

All three changes appear essential to each school's success. The pressure to improve standards has led some school leaders to concentrate only on the second: to use a top–down approach to implement a utilitarian, results driven programme. In so doing they are replicating the government's approach, thereby intensifying the pressures and accompanying stress on staff. For the case study heads, collaboration, in the form of staff working together and supporting each other in pursuit of a shared educational vision, formed an essential element of the reshaped culture. The heads themselves were able to apply pressure in particular situations that required it. But they saw their main task as one of providing support, confidence and guidance that would sustain dedicated and skilled members of staff working in challenging times.

Summary

- ◆ The case study heads were passionate believers in the transforming power of education.
- ◆ They used their passionate beliefs to create a convincing and compelling vision for the future and this helped to secure the commitment of their staff.
- ◆ In doing this, and in moving the school towards the vision, the heads made use of a wide range of leadership styles. This had a positive effect on the organisational climate and hence on the school's performance in its broadest sense. The school was a good place to work in: staff were energised and inspired to give of their best.
- ◆ The heads were able to use different leadership styles to achieve the intended effect by drawing on their spiritual, cognitive and emotional intelligences.
- ◆ Their spiritual intelligence invested their work and that of the school with significance and meaning. Their cognitive intelligence provided them with the analytical tools to move the school forward. Through their emotional intelligence, they were able to take staff with them on the journey towards the better future.
- ◆ The heads encouraged their staff to hold on to their values, to renew their personal vision and develop their professional expertise. They also used external pressures to reshape the teacher-culture of autonomy to include elements of hierarchical accountability and, crucially, in a period of rapid change and uncertainty, collaboration.

Overview

We can never be sure what the full consequences of our decisions will be. No matter how positively we approach a situation, or how thorough and systematic our thinking, unpredictable circumstances or events will always occur. The experienced researcher is used to **confounding variables** – unexpected influences that confound an investigation – and he/she tries to control the influence of these variables using randomisation and other techniques. The experienced manager will also be aware of likely 'gremlins' that may come along to spoil a plan or the expected rate of progress with a project, but the scope to circumvent or compromise may be more limited. We have to accept that 'confounding' or 'chaos' will always occur. We can then try to build in 'lookouts' and arrange contingency plans.

This compensatory process may be helped by considering case scenarios of things that went wrong because of unexpected circumstances, insufficient foresight or intransigence by one or more key leaders. The following 'black spots' are intended to illustrate these risks. Consider each scenario in turn and note down what steps might be taken to prevent the negative consequences recurring in another school.

Over-reliance on one style of leadership

'Followers do not usually go any farther than their leaders.'

Anonymous

An 11–18 school fed by a large run-down suburban estate: In 1994 OFSTED noted that 23% of the pupils achieved five A–C passes at GCSE. By 1998 A*–C GCSEs had fallen to 18%. They were to fall to 16% in 1999. Shortly afterwards the school went into special measures and the headteacher of many years standing resigned.

An interview with the head early in 1999 provided an insight into the culture that had been established:

> 'I'm proud of the excellent relationships within the school. Many of our pupils come from desperately poor home backgrounds and they are not going to be able to cope with the demands of an academic curriculum. If we can teach them to behave in a civilised manner towards each other, then we can consider to have done well. . . . The kind of GCSE results being demanded are just not realistic.'

This head was a very popular figure with his staff, but his emphasis on an 'affiliative' style of leadership (see Chapter 2) accompanied by low expectations of pupil performance, led to results that were well below those achieved by many other schools with similar, and worse, intakes.

Over-reliance on one style of leadership – the 'affiliative' – has meant that 'relationships' were the focus rather than learning. Ironically, the outcome was not the harmony sought: pupil behaviour worsened and staff increasingly found themselves confronting indiscipline as well as poor work.

Pitfalls of location

Dr Vernon
Coleman

> 'Always try to design with people in mind.'

This school embarked on a building programme that resulted, *inter alia*, in a new administration block. Excellent as these facilities were, the effect of locating both the main school office and the headteacher's office in a separate block proved highly damaging. Pupils were allowed to enter the block only for a specific purpose, and the result was that the office staff, who in most schools establish important 'non-teacher' relationships with pupils, became cut off from the main activity of the school. If this were not bad enough, the isolation of the headteacher proved disastrous, with both staff and pupils rarely seeing him.

The absence of a head on site was highly damaging within the school, where relationships between staff and pupils, and between some staff and senior management, reached a state of virtual breakdown. Even worse was the impact on the local catchment area (and eventually on recruitment), with an increasing number of incidents between pupils from this school and those from neighbouring schools.

With both the head and the office staff physically removed from pupils and from the rest of staff, it became impossible to sustain 'teamwork'. In particular, there was no visible senior management team providing a role model for other teams in the schools. In addition, links between the office staff and other support staff were weak and support staff became isolated.

Living in the past

'Things ain't what they used to be and probably never were.'

Will Rogers

An ex-selective boys' school enjoyed an excellent reputation for some time after it went comprehensive. However, a decline in results started to manifest itself until, some five years after the end of selection, the GCSE pass rate was running at the average for the LEA. Such a decline is, of course, not unusual in schools that change their character dramatically. But in this case it continued until the retirement of the head, who had been in post for some twenty years and who had overseen the transfer to all-ability. At this point there was an opportunity for the governors to give tangible recognition to the fact that the school had changed and now needed, albeit belatedly, to re-focus. Sadly, the opportunity was not taken, and the long-standing first deputy was appointed. A measure of his attachment to the school's increasingly irrelevant past was that the tour of the school often failed to get past his office, with its dark oak panelling and plethora of shields and cups reminding all who entered of former glories.

There were two major contributory factors in this school's decline. First, the governing body, because of the influence of two particularly strong personalities who had been associated with the school since its grammar school heyday, failed to respond to the changed circumstances of the school. Second, the 'new' head lacked some essential characteristics that are found in highly effective headteachers, for example, the ability to understand, respond to and shape external pressures and the ability to be proactive and do things ahead of time.

Hero-innovation

'I don't have ulcers, I give them.'

Harry Cohen

A school located in the middle of a residential area of semi-detached and detached houses: Were the school able to recruit from its immediate area, it would be able to achieve a balanced intake. However, most parents in the catchment area choose to send their children to private or selective schools. The school has for many years found it difficult to recruit its standard number, and this has proved an extremely challenging task for the three most recent headteachers.

Any head taking on such a challenge will need a very clear vision, and strategies to implement that vision. The present incumbent's predecessor certainly had 'personal impact and presence' (one of the attributes identified by the DFES as part of the national standards for headteachers) but was unable to take staff with him. His approach was based closely on the 'superhead' concept, with its over-reliance on the head's ability to effect change by her/himself. Policy decisions in this school were more likely to be made by the head than put through senior management or referred to the staff as a whole. The head's relationships with pupils mirrored this autocratic approach. For example, he always insisted that pupils should stand up when he walked into a classroom. This behaviour was not demanded by other staff, and although the head was clearly asserting his presence, he was also risking – and did indeed encounter – a degree of confrontation from staff and from pupils who failed to show due obeisance.

As we saw in Chapter 2: 'managers motivated by personal power are not good institution builders'. The head of this school had little trust in his colleagues and, therefore, found it hard to secure their commitment to changing the school's performance in what were highly challenging circumstances. An additional factor was that the style of the chair of governors was similar to the head's, and they tended to reinforce each other's inappropriate behaviour.

The games people play

Anonymous

'In looking over people, you find there are a lot you would rather overlook.'

Another 'difficult' school that was set in the heart of a decaying industrial area that had suffered from some years with declining rolls and poor results: The head, previously acting head of another school in the same LEA, had a reputation for being 'tough'. However, he had not bargained with a highly opinionated and interventionist chair of governors who wanted, and was able, to visit the school regularly. Unfortunately, the grey boundary between the role of the head and the role of the governing body was not identified until too late, by which time a number of major areas of management had become battlegrounds. One obvious point of conflict was staffing, where the head's professional knowledge and skills were largely ignored. Another was finance, where, because of problems the school had had in the past, significant budgeting decisions were taken against the head's advice.

The extent to which the chair overstepped his role is best illustrated by his involvement in the writing of the school timetable. This was the responsibility of one of the deputies, but the chair of governors would insist on being told when a timetabling session was to take place and would then want to contribute to the process itself!

Heads need to understand how school groups (including the governing body) relate to each other and how to manage them effectively. The head in this situation needed to focus much more closely on shaping this vital relationship with the chair of governors so that the education of pupils, and the school as a whole would benefit. Instead, he saw the conflict as a power battle. This attitude meant there would be no 'winners'.

Careless concessions

'Look twice before you leap.'

Charlotte Brontë

A school in an authority that was generally considered fairly affluent but contained pockets of deprivation: Like others described in this section, this school had traditionally had difficulty recruiting and was considered a 'last resort' by the parents of most children. A typical downward spiral developed, whereby the more unpopular the school became, the less parents chose it for their children and the more vulnerable it became to pressure to take pupils no one else wanted or had room for. The LEA, in its desperation to place their floating population of pupils, increasingly used the school as a 'dumping ground'. Meanwhile, through the heroic efforts of staff, the school started to acquire a reputation for dealing with children with a variety of special needs. This reputation attracted and deterred potential entrants in equal measure, although the overall effect was to establish an intake that was significantly skewed towards the less able.

Finally agreement was reached between the governing body and the LEA to provide facilities in the school for pupils with physical disabilities. A behavioural unit was also established. The net result was that the LEA had a school in which it was easy to place children with a variety of special needs, but the school itself became even more unpopular with all but a small minority of parents whose children's needs could not be met elsewhere.

As with previous examples, there was a failure to 'read' the environment correctly or to understand the interactions taking place within the community around the school. The children with special needs were not, on the whole, those who lived in the immediate catchment area of the school, and local parents were not, on the whole, supportive of the changing profile of the intake. Before bowing to LEA pressure, there should have been much greater analysis of current and projected intakes around the school and in the LEA as a whole.

Undoing the never done

'If you don't think co-operation is necessary, watch what happens to a wagon if one wheel comes off.'

Anonymous

The head of this inner-city school had been off work for a lengthy period and returned to work only to find that the 80–90% fitness he had recovered was insufficient to enable him to cope with the daily rigours of headship. He was then off sick for a year before finally resigning. During this year the school was run by an acting head with no previous experience of senior management. His was as steep a learning curve as it would be possible to find. First, the school was heavily in the red with no real prospect of emerging from debt in the foreseeable future. Second, with exam results well below the average for a school with its particular profile, the impending OFSTED inspection posed a real threat, with the likelihood of – at best – serious weaknesses being identified.

As much as any other factor, it was what the acting head learned about the way the school had been run by his predecessor that helped him develop. First, he had inherited a school development plan that had been written entirely by the head. It was so lengthy and so full of unrealistic and generalised targets that it would have taken a decade to implement. Second, he inherited a school with no staffroom because his predecessor didn't want staff talking to each other. Third, there was an absence of any formal structure for meetings.

This had been another head with little trust in, or respect for, his colleagues, and in this case there was no real belief in teamwork or in the use of a democratic style. The result was the 'central task of the leader' (see Chapter 2) – creating and securing a vision that 'excites the enthusiasm and secures the commitment of its members' – could not be achieved. It is likely that the head's remote and mistrustful style set up tensions that can only have served to raised everyone's stress levels.

As a postscript it is worth mentioning that when the acting head started to involve staff (including setting up a staffroom) a much more positive atmosphere was created. And the OFSTED inspection, when it finally came, recognised the progress the school was making and lifted the threat of condemnation.

Keeping it in the family

> 'If one synchronised swimmer drowns – don't the rest drown too?'

Internet graffiti

A school in a typical urban area in that there was the potential for a mixed intake from the combination of estates, terraced housing and more middle-class residential properties: Until relatively recently the head managed to combine the establishment of liberal values with a rigorous approach to pupil achievement. So, for example, the school's equal opportunities policy had been worked through numerous staff and pupil committees and was considered to be at the heart of the school's operations. The school council and accompanying year councils were given great prominence, and pupil involvement in the life and running of the school, including staff appointments, was significant. The arts were invested in heavily. There was no 'sloppy liberalism'. There was a structure and purpose that gave the school a feeling of a very together community.

Eventually the head, in whose time the above developments had taken place, moved to another post and was replaced by his deputy. It quickly became clear that the school ethos and the culture of tolerance and appreciation had been established through hard work rather than woolly notions of collegiality. The new head assumed that the good relations operating throughout the school would sustain themselves. Sadly, this was far from the truth and very soon ragged edges began to appear. School concerts that had previously been highly organised showpieces for pupil talent became less formal, with fewer rehearsals and less respectful audiences. The pupil councils met less regularly. The concept of equal opportunities which had seemed so ingrained, became more of an issue.

Results started to suffer. The school started a descent from which it would take four years to recover.

The original head had displayed the full range of leadership styles described in Chapter 2. In particular, he employed the **authoritative style** in order to create a long-term vision for the school to which all members of the school community subscribed. His use of the democratic and affiliative styles was also highly visible. The succeeding head did not have the same sense of conviction and thus was unable to use the authoritative style to such effect. He also failed to understand how the coercive, the pace-setting and the coaching styles were also necessary in order to maintain standards of achievement and clarity of purpose.

Lost opportunities

Erica Jong

> 'And the trouble is if you don't risk anything, you risk even more.'

One of OFSTED's main findings on re-inspecting this primary school was its failure to act on a number of action points from the last inspection. In particular, the school had no effective system of self-evaluation, had made little progress towards performance management and had not been able to set up a satisfactory programme of staff development (including almost no effective provision for the induction of new staff).

The school acted as the main feeder for a very successful and hugely oversubscribed secondary on its doorstep, but inspectors noted that no ongoing links had been established with this secondary school. Staff confided that they were keen to respond to frequent initiatives from the secondary school but felt that their headteacher would not support them if they did.

The primary headteacher had been in post for nearly twenty years. Whilst in the early years of her headship she had tried to open up what had traditionally been a very 'insular' school, latterly she appeared to have lost interest. From the perspective of staff, inertia had reached the point of obstruction.

This school had been 'coasting' over a long period. Initially, its secure catchment area and the fact that families moved into that area in order to get their children into the nearby secondary school meant that it was not at risk. However, over a period of years, as other local primary schools developed and improved, the head and her staff appeared to be increasingly out of touch. The head in particular no longer took initiatives and tended to operate reactively rather than proactively. Most significantly, she was no longer tuned to the voices of parents and of the community immediately around the school – all of whom were clearly indicating their dissatisfaction with the education the school was now providing.

Broken halo

> 'You can only predict things after they've taken place.'

Eugene Ionesco

A long-standing headteacher presiding over a highly successful primary school that regularly obtains excellent results decided to get feedback from staff on their perceptions of the school and of his leadership style (very much on the lines of the DFES's 'Leadership Programme for Serving Headteachers'). He had been a teacher for fifteen years and had been wondering whether to carry on until he could retire (in four years) or look for a second headship. His plans received a serious jolt when he got some very negative feedback from staff. They felt he was remote, didn't acknowledge and reward their efforts and didn't give them sufficient responsibility.

This headteacher is not alone in being surprised by negative feedback. There are two factors at work here. First, being head of a 'successful' school over a long period of time tends to breed complacency – a kind of 'What more do we need to do to prove ourselves?' attitude. Schools with relatively advantaged intakes could, until the end of the last century, feel reasonably confident that their results would show them in a favourable light. However, with the advent of increasingly sophisticated 'value-added' analyses, such schools are having to prove 'added value' rather than simply rely on talented intakes. Second, as so often happens in small schools, the head becomes the fulcrum, or focal point, for all the school's activities, and staff are increasingly sidelined in terms of policy. The result is staff who not only feel they have no responsibility but who, because they know nothing else, don't want responsibility. As they stop developing, the school ceases to make progress.

Summary

In general, these black spots indicate a number of important issues about leadership and change:

◆ Leadership must be real to matter.

◆ Leadership must be accessible and visible; it must link with the strategic and operational heart of the school.

◆ Leadership is not merely a delivery mechanism – you can't simply carry out someone else's blueprint.

◆ No team or organisation can live in the past.

◆ Carrying on regardless is not usually a successful strategy.

◆ The isolated or heroic style of leadership has little validity in complex situations.

◆ Part of the task of leadership may be to block unwise decisions before wise ones can be made.

◆ Good leader-managers spend a lot of time on external and sideline relationships.

◆ Leaders cannot assume effectiveness; they must listen and respond.

Overview

Some schools just go on getting better whilst others enjoy occasional success but are inclined to alternate their steps forwards with frequent steps backwards. This chapter examines the ingredients of peak performance – in particular how to get the best out of as many of your staff as possible without burning them and yourself out. It also considers the damaging roles played by marginal performers and looks at what can be done – at worst to limit their impact, at best to improve their performance.

Managing for peak performance

'The statue is already in the rock. My job is to cut away surplus stone.'   Michelangelo

Peak performance in schools depends on successfully interlocking a number of factors:

◆ knowing what constitutes 'peak performance' for students, staff and the school as a whole;
◆ understanding oneself and how one works best and reaches 'best work';
◆ knowing what brings out the best in those you lead and manage.

Definition

'Peak' suggests 'summit'. The difference between 'peak' as in performance and 'peak' as in summit is that the former knows no bounds, whereas the latter is finite. However, even in mountaineering circles, someone who has been brought up to think of Everest as the ultimate achievement may well seek new, more demanding challenges, once she/he has climbed it.

We do not know what limits there are to human achievement. There is only a continual river of potential, and the daily stories of success against all odds, or against all expectations, can only lead us to conclude that 'anything is possible'.

It is frustrating both for students and for their teachers that every time results in public examinations exceed the previous best, there are attempts to discredit the improved performance. In nearly all other spheres of human endeavour, the expected norm is that progress will be made. For example, an athlete's improved running time, more accurate weather forecasting, developments in the quantification of a medical condition and better client satisfaction figures in a public service are all seen as positive outcomes. In contrast, the idea that children just might be getting cleverer and working harder, or that teachers might be teaching better, appears hard for some to accept (particularly opposition politicians and some of those who did well in yesterday's system).

Those who wish to encourage peak performance will ignore the sceptics and press on to higher ground. They will concentrate on focusing their energy on success for the individual and, through that, success for their school and for themselves. For students know when they have done well, and so do their parents. Both groups also know that this seldom happens without teachers and support staff working to **their** peak performance. This has to be in relation to all activities – from results in public exams, to punctuality, to the speedy removal of litter and graffiti.

Peak performance for students

For the great majority of teachers a passionate belief in what students can achieve is the force that drives them forward. It may well be that, like the headteachers in some of the case studies outlined in Chapter 3, part of the reason they came into teaching was their own experiences as students – either successfully overcoming the odds, or failing at the school stage but reflecting subsequently on what might have been. For many, the quality of the education they received at school gave them a lifetime love of learning that they later desired to pass on to others.

However, despite the fact that two people may enter teaching for similar ideological reasons and begin their careers with the same positive aspirations, they will discover that maintaining students' motivation through good teaching is not an easy task. The best teachers have off-days and some teachers find it more difficult than others to sustain high levels of professionalism. After starting teaching, most teachers are only too aware of real variance in professional performance. They will see students taught by one member of staff getting excellent results; but the same students taught by a less effective teacher will fail to achieve.

Pupils in 'effective schools' will have their sights raised. They will be given learning targets that stretch their capabilities. They will achieve more than they thought was possible. They will develop new skills and gain increased confidence. Such achievements will inspire not only their teachers but also their peers. The implicit thinking will be 'if she/he can do it, so can I'.

One practical way in which schools prove that some teachers are more effective than others is by comparing the attainment of pupils across subjects. Obviously, some differences come from students' interest/aptitude for particular areas of the curriculum. However, when, for similar groups of students, there are **significant** differences between grades in, say, history and geography, or French and Spanish, then the likelihood is that these differences demonstrate the effectiveness of the teachers responsible for the higher grades. They have motivated and engaged the students in a manner that has sustained learning and achievement. Sammons *et al.* (1997) convincingly explore evidence that successful subject departments in schools achieve results that other colleagues appear unable to secure.

Although the focus here is on performance in public examinations, 'peak performance' for pupils applies more broadly. It should embrace the range of 'clevernesses' referred to by Handy (1996). He identified creativity, musicality, athleticism, practicality, psychic cleverness (seen in 'intuitive' creators such as poets) and 'people cleverness' (the ability to get things done with people). Teachers and schools can, and do, bring out all these capabilities, just as they develop academic intellect. The effective school will not allow the educative process to concentrate on one of these areas at the expense of the others.

Strategic PIN down – Reflection 6.1	**Aims**
	◆ to encourage subject departments to examine the performance of pupils they have taught against the performance of the same pupils taught by other departments;
	◆ to spread best practice across the school.

P – State the PROBLEM   There is insufficient analysis of the performance of pupils in public examinations. To increase reliable evidence we need . . .

| Strategic PIN down – Reflection 6.1 (cont.) | **I** – Clarify the ISSUE | Students' grades differ by significant amounts in subjects where they might be expected to be reasonably close. In our school this is particularly the case . . . |
| | **N** – Tackle the NEED | To encourage departments to carry out their own analyses of results and act on the findings we need to highlight . . . and provide . . . |

Before you begin, think about:

◆ What system is in place for analysing exam results?
◆ How much say have departments had in setting up the system?
◆ Do they think it is fair?
◆ How are the analyses being used? How could they be used?

Tip
Don't make departments construct their own 'tables'. Provide all the basic data in accessible form. Remember, analysis without review and follow-up will be of little worth.

Peak performance in schools

The OFSTED perspective

How does peak performance for students manifest itself in terms of the whole school? How is peak performance at the school level determined and recognised? OFSTED (1999) asks a number of questions that are designed to throw light on these two key issues. First, it suggests the necessity to decide on the chief 'characteristics of the school'. In other words, the judgements made implicitly or explicitly about a school's effectiveness have to be placed within the context of that particular school. Encouragingly, after decades of frustration for high-achieving schools in impoverished circumstances, attempts are being made to better describe and quantify contextual circumstances, and then measure progress from this base in terms of the amount of value added to students' prior attainment.

Second, OFSTED points to the level of the school's performance in overall terms when it asks the: How high are the standards? It then sweeps together a range of information to answer this question. Consideration is given to:

- the results in National Curriculum and other tests;
- the challenge in the performance targets the school has set itself and how far it is on course to meet or exceed them;
- the rate and level of progress being made by different sectors of the student population – in particular, students with special educational needs; those learning through English as an additional language; those with specific gifts and talents; those from minority ethnic groups; and boys compared with girls;
- the school's performance compared with that achieved by similar schools (i.e. an attempt to compare 'like with like');
- any evidence of value added in relation to students' starting points.

In general, a school with high standards is recognised as an effective school, providing those high standards are being achieved within reasonable cost limits, both material and human. However, animated discussion continues around the nature of the judgements made about school performance and their overall fairness. In the final analysis, the extent to which a school is on the road to peak performance, and the attainment or not of its goals, cannot be judged in absolute terms. No one has tablets of stone. What information is pursued and emphasised reflects the political, ideological or professional interests of the data gatherers. Though more agreement is emerging about the most satisfactory holistic perspective on a school's performance, and how far inspection or other evidence provides this, consensus is not yet reached. It is also essential to judge 'peak performance' and general effectiveness in terms of the school's own interpretation of its mission:

'Schools vary in the relative emphasis they place on different types of goals, and in the emphasis they place on different academic subjects. Thus, monitoring systems that measure only a few aspects of academic achievement are likely to misrepresent the performance of some schools.

A related problem is whether monitoring systems emphasise excellence or equity. Schools vary . . . in their allocation of resources to different types of pupils. . . . Care must be taken to ensure that indicators describe a range of levels of performance, and that analyses of data describe the distribution of scores in a school or district, not just average scores.'

Willms 1992, pp. 149–50

The whole child

Many readers will agree with Willms that school performance has a number of facets. They will vary in how far they feel that OFSTED's lines of enquiry align with their own views on what is important. Many teachers feel that whilst the OFSTED approach is a broad one, its fails to capture the joy, satisfaction and stimulation reflected in the very best work done with students. They feel that OFSTED's markers for evaluation reflect only part of the humanitarian goals most schools strive for. Thus, these markers represent only a **part** of the work that effective, high-performing teachers carry out in their schools.

The balance between instrumental and more esoteric goals is not easy to achieve. In the 1960s and 1970s many schools had commendable aims to educate the 'whole child'. Too often, however, this meant that more basic or urgent outcomes were not secure. Some presented a warmth and tolerance that seemed to militate against a learning environment, or which marked them out as pursuing very different educational objectives to their nearest school neighbour. At the end of the 1970s two north London comprehensives exemplified this dilemma: one was seen as a school for students (i.e. they achieved good examination results) and the other was seen as a school for staff (i.e. there was a strong orientation towards the maintenance of good staff relationships whatever the cost, and the 'affiliative style' of leadership was overplayed).

In general, more schools, like the case study examples in Chapter 3, now seek a strong balance between instrumental and broader educational goals. They do not feel they have to be 'Gradgrindish' to educate their students effectively. They recognise that students do need confidence with the basic skills and that they do need to achieve to their academic potential, including the best range of achievement in public examinations. But they see these objectives as possible within a culture that shows students both care and respect and seeks to provide them with opportunities to develop all of their capabilities. They are as liberal as they can be, but in a more focused fashion than some of the 'liberal' establishments of 30 years ago. They answer OFSTED's question – How well are students taught? – by constantly refining their teaching practice, communicating the highest expectations to students, and by monitoring and improving students' learning outcomes.

Distinguishing efficiency from effectiveness

It is important to distinguish between 'effective' and 'efficient' performance. Efficient might, quite acceptably, imply an aeroplane operating at its cruising altitude with a perfect balance existing between speed and fuel consumption. Some school managers seem to be able, like the cruising plane, to work at high speed without consuming excessive amounts of energy. That is they operate efficiently on administrative, budget, staff, resource and timetable matters, so that the procedural side of the school works as an organised and understood system. This is because efficiency is primarily about sustaining rationality. In terms of school effectiveness, however, efficiency is not enough. To be effective a school has to be more than efficient. It has to be **valid**. That is, its climate, ethos, teaching and learning, work ethic, staff development and community involvement has to be **worthwhile** in terms of core values that students, parents and the broader society can recognise as humane and beneficial.

This is because schools are complex institutions that reflect significant aspects of the society of which they are a part. To be effective in this sense, schools obviously acknowledge and put in place functional efficiency, but they also strive for more purposeful ends. They seek to be 'fit for purpose' for their students and their place in time and to meet the ethical, political, social and technological goals that are seen by the local and national community as being most important to secure. For the school to be effective the teachers must have a real sense of purpose. They will have more than a love of a subject. They will understand the subject in the round, be able to teach it well and be capable of justifying why it merits curriculum time. Above all, they will have a passion to educate others in its content, skills and values. They will also love and value children and therefore wish to see that the manner and means by which they address the subject helps them to apply learning in a way that benefits students' lives.

To return to the flying analogy, Blanchard (1994) describes the efficient pilot making perfect take-offs and landings. The effective pilot, however, cares about her/his passengers to the point where she/he plans an informative journey and keeps an eye on the navigation to ensure arrival at the right airport.

The role of the headteacher

The arrangements whereby so-called 'superheads' are put in charge of schools where significant change is needed are not proving successful. The fashion is to trust charismatic and individual 'leadership' over more fundamental management structures, including having strong arrangements for team working. However, this belief is foundering, as the 'hero-innovators' do not seem to be able to achieve what needs to be achieved. This is not surprising, as the weakness of this approach, i.e. trusting in the myth of the hero-innovator, has been made clear on many earlier occasions (see, for example, Georgiades and Phillimore 1975).

Whilst there should be an appropriate emphasis on the talents and skills of the individual at the head of the institution (in order to secure the success of that institution), research indicates that such success cannot be achieved single-handedly. Success appears to come from heads who seek to 'steer', more than from those who wish to be the main or only 'driver'. In short, effective collective leadership is crucial to a school's development.

Drucker (1970) describes the managing director of a highly successful multinational company who never worried about his own role in the generation of ideas. He knew that, amongst the top managers in the company, there would never be any shortage of ideas. Though the reader who is head of a small primary school with one ineffectual deputy may smile at this, the message is still a powerful one. A headteacher cannot meet all the demands of a multifaceted role. There has to be delegation to colleagues, trust of those colleagues to do the job right, and humility about one's own contribution in the light of the achievement of the team as a whole. Important aspects of teamwork are explored in Chapter 7.

The performance of each headteacher will be affected by a number of factors. Amongst these will be:

◆ how far there is match between the school hosting the headship and the dispositions and talents of the potential leader (hopefully a visit and interview will enable would-be applicants to consider and answer such questions as: Is this the job I really want? Or is it just any headship? Is it doable? Can I cope **in this context** with the pressures identified in the survey by NAHT (2000)? – e.g. OFSTED inspection, bureaucracy, governors and governors meetings, abusive or violent parents, levels of underfunding);

◆ the ability to recognise self-capabilities and shortcomings, in order to use the first and compensate for the second;

◆ the extent to which heads can see and utilise the capabilities of others – staff, students, governors, parents, LEA and local community representatives, volunteers, etc.;

◆ the repertoire of leadership skills that can be applied confidently and flexibly by each head (see again Chapters 2–4);

◆ the choice of initial moves or changes and how far these get the head 'off on the right foot':

> 'change . . . engages both intellect and emotions; it may impinge on people's value systems; it not only affects individuals but also the organisation, its structures, its norms and its environment. Consequently it will not happen successfully unless it is promoted, steered or facilitated with all these crucial factors being taken into account.'

Everhard and
Morris 1985, p. xi

Notice board 3   Headship in some contexts

A new head, or one transferring from one headship to another, may meet a situation drawn from this wide spectrum of scenarios:

◆ new school – 'greenfield' site, with a year from appointment to opening (rare, but still possible);

◆ new school – existing buildings but no staff or pupils;

◆ new school – existing buildings, staff and pupils, change in name and new head;

◆ existing school – well established, successful, with dynamic predecessor moving on to 'higher things';

◆ existing school – well established, successful, long-standing previous headship (15+ years), some complacency among staff, to use current jargon, school is 'coasting';

◆ existing school – generally recognised as having gone downhill but not yet at crisis point;

◆ existing school – either at or near failure/serious weaknesses, as judged by OFSTED.

Notice board 3   Headship in some contexts (cont.)

Each situation requires a different approach on the part of the incoming head. Care will have to be taken in approaching staff, deciding on any changes in roles and responsibilities, and beginning an initial development plan or revitalising an established one. Though some experienced heads are sufficiently flexible and have a sufficiently wide range of leadership styles to operate effectively in any one of these or other contexts, this will not always be the case. It is also dangerous to assume that an approach that produces success in one school will produce success in another. It may pay to be upfront about any reservations. For example, a candidate for a secondary headship in the south of England in 1999 surprised one of the selection panels by announcing that the school was heading for serious financial difficulties. Initial reaction was hostile and defensive, but the candidate was able to back his assertion with a detailed analysis of the problem. He was eventually offered the job and accepted it. At least, in part, he knew what he was taking on. He had registered initial concern and begun to prioritise actions.

An effective appointment process should assist the first stage of engaging staff in securing 'peak performance'. This is because an effective process will have involved some staff, and perhaps a significant number of governors, in the appointment. They will have listened to each candidate's views and the answers to specific questions. Most importantly, it is likely they will have been exposed to each candidate's educational philosophy. They will, therefore, have some idea about what the selected applicant stands for (and possibly won't stand for). All these people have a stake in ensuring the success of the person appointed. The individual selected for the job will have strong support from them. They will hold pluses for the new head and – providing the 'new broom' can chalk up, and publicise, some early success – they will expect continued progress, not failure. They are anticipating 'peak performance'. The stage is set.

Strategic PIN down – Reflection 6.2	**Aims**
	◆ to understand that each new post, whether in your current school or a new one, will require a specific approach;
	◆ to consider further the repertoire of leadership styles.

P – State the PROBLEM	We tend towards the view that we have a 'natural' way of operating that needs little adaptation from one job to another. This can restrict professional development because . . .
I – Clarify the ISSUE	School situations vary greatly according to their current staff, their history and the particular issues facing them. The leadership team need an accurate knowledge of the school context. It is essential in order to . . .
N – Tackle the NEED	In order to deal with a wide range of new and recurring management situations, school leaders need awareness of the widest possible range of leadership styles. This awareness is best developed . . .

Before you begin, think about:

◆ your initial analysis of each new job you have taken on and how accurate it was;

◆ what information you gathered to prepare yourself for a new role;

◆ what initial action you planned;

◆ how successful you were in making an initial impact. Where you had most success and why?

◆ what effect the initial impact had on your subsequent successes and problems.

Tip

Look at some professional role models (good and bad) from your current and previous experience. Examine some relevant literature on examples of effective leadership (e.g. Adair (1997) and Gronn (1999)).

Managing staff in the role of new headteacher

Anonymous

> 'Seek to impress not express.'

The initial impact

Notice board 4   Headship through virtual reality

A CD-ROM produced for the first version of the NPQH (National Professional Qualification for Headship) training programme is called 'Practising Leadership'. It simulates the situation a newly appointed headteacher finds herself/himself in from day one of the autumn term. Those using it for the first time tend to struggle with the technology and find they are getting regular phone calls and memos from staff on the lines of: 'Headteacher, it is now nearly the end of the second week (first month/first half-term/first term, etc.) and staff would very much like to meet you to find out your thinking on the future direction of the school.' Whilst the CD-ROM allows you to go back and start again, real life is not so forgiving.

Very careful thought needs to be given to:

◆ handling the initial impact on staff;
◆ defining the style of approach – i.e. the balance across telling, selling, coercing and cajoling;
◆ setting out any visionary ideas;
◆ establishing the nature and the direction of decision-making;
◆ deciding who to involve in any new actions, at what points and in what ways;
◆ outlining timescales in which any tasks are expected to be done;
◆ defining the expected protocols and procedures for consultation ('open door' at one end, observance of defined line-management arrangements at the other).

From the outset you will need to make clear – either explicitly or through more subtle means – your expectations of all students and staff with regard to fundamentals such as respect for others, responsible behaviour, hard work and working together.

Much will then depend on the nature of the context you are taking over. For example, going back to the scenarios listed on Notice board 3, your approach to 'existing school – well established, successful, with dynamic predecessor moving on to higher things' will be quite different from your approach to 'existing school – generally recognised as having gone downhill but not yet at crisis point'.

In the first scenario a degree of humility, of 'getting the feel of things', would be appropriate; in the second, it is likely that the majority of staff – especially given the enthusiastic fanfare with which your appointment was greeted – would be hoping for, and expecting, some fairly rapid action.

One of the authors of this book was drafted in as acting head of a secondary school to take over from a head who had resigned on the last day of the summer term. The school appeared to be in a state of crisis and in need of root-and-branch reform. On closer examination, the new head realised that the problem was concentrated at the top, where relations had broken down between the key stakeholders. While blood was being spilt on the executive carpet, staff had kept their heads down and got on with what they had to do. The teaching was of a very high standard, the students responded well, and there was an orderly and positive atmosphere in the school. What staff needed was recognition of what they were doing and affirmation of its (and their) value; what the school needed was a sense of strategic direction.

Whatever the situation, appealing to the middle ground is a useful strategy to sustain. This will, of course, depend on the nature of the staff you inherit (assuming you are not taking over a new school), but, generally speaking, there will be a 'bell curve' representing staff responsiveness. At one end there will be a minority of enthusiasts likely to embrace anything that looks progressive. At the other end will be the cynics who have seen it all before and who know that whatever it is you want to do will (a) not work or (b) require increased effort, which is unacceptable. (For 'middle ground' you can often read 'silent majority', because both the extreme groups tend to be vocal.)

Initial contact with the Senior Management Team

You will have the governors (or at least the majority of them) 'onside' via the appointment process. Staff expectations are positive, but as yet you have not spoken to them directly; nor have you spoken to your Senior

Management Team (SMT). This is almost certainly where you should start. Just as your relationship with your chair of governors will be crucial to your job satisfaction and effectiveness, so will it be with the relationship with your senior management colleagues. These are the people with whom you will be in daily contact, on whom you will have to rely in order for the school to run successfully. Your relationship with them will provide a role model for all other teams in the school. Above all, taking these colleagues into your confidence and trust will provide a secure base from which your vision can be shared and disseminated.

Peak performance has to be stimulated and demonstrated by the headteacher. Equally clearly, peak performance has to be shown by and supported by the individuals and teams you are responsible for. There is so much work that has to be done in schools that delegation needs to be real and trust needs to be total if the 'synergy' of total teamwork is to result in peak performance.

The first staff meeting

Barring unforeseen circumstances, you will be chairing a staff meeting on the first day of your first term. This needs to be at the start of the day in order that you, and the rest of your staff, set the tone for what should be the next phase of the school's life. But what about your senior colleagues? They will have a crucial role not only in the implementation of the changes that your appointment will inevitably trigger but also, equally importantly, in the sharing and dissemination of the vision. Will you **tell** them what you are going to say to staff and defy comment? Will you **show them** a summary of the points you are going to make and await reactions? Or will you **talk through** your speech to staff and ask for comments? Your ability to communicate and stick to a 'vision' for the school, and at the same time to be open and open-minded about its reasonableness and potential, will have a major impact on the extent to which your best colleagues will be drawn into its realisation.

Tackling a major issue

Assume that you have identified 'low expectations' as a major issue to tackle. This is likely to be low **staff** expectations of students, leading to students having low expectations of themselves. The **key to change** will lie in the extent to which you are able to change staff perceptions and staff behaviour. In order to 'depersonalise' the issue you will probably find yourself talking about students' expectations when discussing the issue with staff as a whole, i.e. talking about student achievement and student potential. However, within the senior management team you may be able to tackle the root of the problem more directly.

Schools that have established a structure for monitoring students' work are likely to have more direct evidence of the effects of different expectations. For example, samples of students' work across subjects can be examined term by term. Initially, the focus will be on what the exercise is telling staff about students. However, it will not be long before patterns of teacher practice start to emerge – homework not set, books not marked, poor work accepted, insufficient feedback to students, too much incomplete work, etc. The focus then shifts to the action needed to improve teachers' use and handling of learning activities and learning tasks, and the way they use students' work for monitoring and diagnostic purposes. Inevitably, senior staff will need to consider how the best practice with students and the best use of their work can be replicated across the whole school.

Issues in focus 6.1

It is important to involve all staff in discussing the aims behind sampling collections of students' work and the type of analysis that will be undertaken. Fundamental questions that need to be addressed are:

◆ For the purposes of the exercise, what range of students' work will be examined? (If only written work or exercise books are scrutinised, what are the advantages and disadvantages of this focus and what message does it give to staff and students?)
◆ How will the examination be carried out and by whom? (Will only full sets of work be included – for example, all the work done for a particular topic or module?)
◆ What steps will be taken to ensure that the sample of work is representative of the general output?
◆ Will students be involved in the exercise? (For example, talking through their work and their reactions to it.)
◆ Most significantly, how will the analysis contribute to managing teachers' practice and teachers' continuing professional development? ↓

Jones and Sparks (1996), McCall (1998) and Woods and Orlik (1994) consider some of these questions and others. The OFSTED inspection handbook (1999) also offers helpful criteria. To emphasise the managerial and professional development value of analysing students' work, it may also be useful to employ the strategy of 'forward' and 'backward' mapping. This strategy relates to many aspects of professional practice (see Field *et al*. 2000). A broader development than simply analysing students' work is the 'collective review' of classroom craft (Brighouse and Woods 1999).

Appropriate use of leadership style

How successful you are in sustaining your early messages will depend on how you match your leadership style to the management situations facing you. If you are serious about staff involvement and you genuinely respect your colleagues (who, you need to remember, are your intellectual and professional peers), then you will wish to check their responses to different types of approach – such as rational argument, brainstorming and coaching or mentoring through to a solution. Thus, a significant question might be: Can I win this target setting argument through rational means? For example, you want to raise GCSE targets by 20%. There are reservations. Can you demonstrate, through example and discussion, that this is a realistic figure? If you can't, then no amount of argument is likely to break through.

Encountering resistance

Where too many staff are operating below an acceptable level, there may be a need, in the initial stages, for more carrot than stick. But care must be taken not to generate a dependency culture whereby staff do what they are told – but without enthusiasm or commitment. If you generate this culture – as many headteachers in desperate attempts to pull up their schools do – you lose your colleagues' creativity and energy. The Bridge Market case study in Chapter 3 is a good example of getting the balance right. The newly appointed headteacher needed to launch an immediate and rigorous assault on underperformance. Though retaining her 'sticking points', the head also demonstrated a capacity to adapt her leadership style as improvement began to emerge. The developing success was 'owned' by all the staff, and the head took over a steering rather than a driving role.

We have suggested that in many schools it is reasonable to assume that staff enthusiasm and commitment will represent a crude 'bell curve'. Your aim will be to break this up by getting **all** staff 'onside'. It may be at first reasonable and rational to aim at the 'middle ground', but you must not ignore the ends of the spectrum. It is important to consider how best to involve the enthusiasts – especially those who are genuinely 'two steps ahead' – while justifying actions to the sceptical and showing them any evidence of early success. Despite what might be difficult responses, it is important to keep open the doors of 'regular information', 'consultation' and 'negotiation'. Though some staff may not agree with certain policy decisions and directions, if you are as open as possible, they cannot 'rubbish the action by default' – i.e. claim they did not know what was going on.

Getting it to be 'our school'

If you are establishing a positive, purposeful and successful school culture, the message is taken on by staff and students that the school is 'theirs', not 'yours'. For some headteachers, the idea of handing over the school and its culture through delegation and shared actions is hard to embrace. This may be because of a desire for self-aggrandisment, in which case it is likely that pride will precede a fall. It may be because they genuinely believe that if an initiative is not associated with them its impact will be lessened. A salutary example was the incidence of the infamous 'leaked memos' that served to undermine 'New Labour' in the first half of the year 2000. These suggested the prime minister insisted on being **personally associated** with all major initiatives. If true, the approach denies the value and power of synergy:

> 'Senior managers routinely doom change initiatives by investing too much of themselves in them. The idea quickly becomes equated with the individual, complicating the picture for the unpersuaded. It's great when the executive in question is universally admired and revered. But that is seldom the case. Too many leaders see managed change as their legacy, like Stalin's Five-Year Plans. Allow daylight to creep between you and your idea. Any change that is inseparable from the leader who puts it in play has little chance of success.'

Robbins and Finley
1997, p. 111

A particular satisfying example of ownership 'disseminated and appropriated' came from one headteacher in the Midlands when, at the end of an interview for an internal post, the candidate (who had been on the staff for some five years) suddenly launched into a detailed analysis and representation of 'our school's way'. What the headteacher and senior managers in the school still considered to be a largely 'top–down' culture had in fact been appropriated by staff.

So 'peak performance' will come from the ability of the leader/top manager to tap that potential for being motivated that all staff have within them – and this means operating McGregor's (1960) Theory X and Theory Y approach (see p. 129).

Of course, as we have already shown, some staff will always be doubters or reticent about change. But don't give up on them. Continue to treat their views with respect. Always look for opportunities to draw them in. A genuine convert, especially one with a loud voice in the staffroom, is worth a great deal.

Issues in focus 6.2

In the first book in this series (McCall and Lawlor 2000) we explored the purposes and potential of self-managed teams. The establishment and encouragement of such teams can be a valuable 'rapport builder' for a new head who wants to phase in a programme of justified change.

Chang and Curtin (1994) assert that moving people from doubt and dependency to a willingness to be involved in self-management and self-managed teams depends on certain strategies. These include:

◆ thinking through and 'publicising' the benefits of self-management;
◆ using exemplars to show how self-managed teams have more operational flexibility to make the right decisions and act on them;
◆ setting the stage for making the concept of self-managed teams a reality within your organisation;
◆ analysing readiness;
◆ agreeing the team's 'key' responsibilities;
◆ establishing 'team transition' plans – e.g. a cross-subject or cross-sector training plan;
◆ agreeing how the team will interact as a team and with other teams, including the most senior managers;
◆ creating clear action plans for initial projects;
◆ communicating the effect of self-managed teams on the organisation as a whole.

Recognising achievement

The most effective institutions generate a culture of appreciation. However, such appreciation, if it is not to be tokenistic, must be team-based or individualised and must relate to real achievement. Though the great majority of students are keen to do well and have their achievements recognised, they also hate to be patronised with false praise. Most professionals are the same.

In an organisation like a school, the extent to which staff feel that appreciation is devalued relates to the amount of praise meted out *en bloc*. The morning after a successful school production it is all too easy to thank everyone who was involved or took part – and ignore the fact that some who contributed did far less than they had originally promised, while others greatly exceeded what was expected of them. Such blanket 'thank-yous' and 'congratulations' do have their place, but they need to be backed up by **individual** expressions of appreciation. Conversely, overpraising an individual for what was achieved by a team is equally demotivating.

Any public or private correspondence relating to appreciation and praise should, whenever possible, help to re-emphasise the school's core values and practice: 'This demonstrates what we believe.' 'This shows how well we do things.' (See case study on Orchard School, Chapter 3). Every opportunity should be taken to relay key messages – from informal conversations with individuals and daily briefings to the larger 'set-piece' events such as open evenings, parent workshops and staff conferences.

Similarly, all written communications can reinforce key principles and reflect the expected tone. Individual notes to members of staff with thanks or congratulations, school newsletters and reports to governors can all 'fly the flag' of what the school is and what it feels about itself. A 'litmus test' measure of how far the 'performance culture' is nourishing the very roots of the school is the extent to which all of the above verbal and written communications are openly undertaken by the widest possible range of staff. Such open communication is often seen in effective schools. They pride themselves on the extent to which positive messages are shared across the entire staff, student and parent populations. The instance of a kitchen supervisor in a struggling northern secondary school who told a visiting inspector that in eight years the headteacher had never once addressed her by name indicates the lack of sensitivity that often prevents any real sense of institutional harmony. One of the authors worked full-time for two-and-a-half years in a large factory. Throughout the entire period he was there written correspondence to him began 'Dear 10048' (his works number). During that time he observed many instances of mature and, on the whole, very honest adults taking every opportunity to subvert the management's and the company's goals. In general, the 'medium' really 'is the message'.

Promoting rigour

Initial progress can start to wane if it is not backed up by target-setting and monitoring structures that become embedded and, therefore, contextualised. Reaching this state of affairs is hard work because these structures are, in effect, saying 'let's challenge ourselves still further', 'let's be uncompromising in assessing our achievements', 'let's check if we are getting where we intended to be'. Too many excellent initiatives die for lack of long-term planning and lack of attention to strategies that might sustain them. Without such structures peak performance will be idiosyncratic. It may manifest itself in fits and starts, but it is unlikely to become habitual. Seeking a rigorous approach to performance means doing agreed things time and time again until they become second nature. Rigour is seen to be part of 'our strength'; it is not the application of some remote and external power to the point of draconian oppression which 'cures the disease but kills the patient'.

Watch the 'burn-out' factor

It is obvious, then, that establishing and sustaining initiatives, both short- and long-term calls for consistent management and leadership skills. There can hardly be a school in the country that couldn't offer numerous examples of developments, intended to be long-term, that turned out to be one-offs. It is easy to understand why so much good work in schools, intended as part of a long-term cycle of change, falls at the first hurdle or drifts into the wayside. Without proper preparation and realistic costing of time and energy, staff become overstretched and cease to be able to function effectively. As indicated in McCall and Lawlor 2000, they can drift into an imbalance whereby they 'live to work' rather than 'work to live'. They may lose the sparkle and commitment to the broader life that it is so necessary to draw on if students are to remain motivated. Thus continually re-examining our projects, their effects on others and their effects on ourselves may be an essential element in preventing burn-out. Many heads consciously or unconsciously model 'workaholism' by being the first to arrive at school each day and the last to leave. They would be better advised to find more economic ways of looking after themselves and their staff. The oft-quoted expression 'work smarter not longer' needs continual recognition and constant examination in the light of each individual's professional responsibilities:

'Behaviour in the workplace has to be re-negotiated all the time. We need to re-negotiate in the light of Equal Opportunities legislation, in the light of new Quality procedures, in the light of recession or boom, European directives, awareness of sexual harassment, integrating new technologies, and a hundred other issues. Reviewing and re-thinking our management style is rewarding because it helps us to meet all these challenges more effectively. It is rewarding because it gives us clues how to drive our energies well without burning out; and finally it is rewarding because it gives us time to reflect not only on the push for success, but also exactly what our personal sense of satisfaction and fulfilment comes from, so that, in the rush of a busy life, we do not wake up one day and find we have lost touch with it.'

O'Brien 1993, p. 5

Strategic PIN down – Reflection 6.3	**Aims**
	◆ to understand the impact of major initiatives and what influences how far they can be sustained;
	◆ to distinguish, in the planning process, between a range of initiatives.

P – State the PROBLEM	Initiatives are launched at great cost in terms of time and energy. Many prove not to be sustainable. They fail because . . .
I – Clarify the ISSUE	Human and material resources must be used at all times to best possible effect. Strategies to maximise effect include . . .
N – Tackle the NEED	To establish planning mechanisms that ensure clear distinctions are made between 'one-offs' and long-term projects, attention needs to be given to . . .

<table>
<tr><td>

Strategic PIN down – Reflection 6.3 (cont.)

</td><td>

Before you begin, think about:

◆ The history of initiatives at your school. What has happened to them?

◆ What mechanisms are in play for introducing new initiatives? When they work – why? When they don't work – why not?

◆ To what extent are new initiatives time-scaled as short- or long-term projects? How are long-term projects started and guided?

◆ Are new initiatives, whether one-offs or long-term, set against all the other activities going on in the school in a planned manner? If so, how is this done?

Tip

Get some feedback from a range of staff on the extent to which they feel that the expenditure of time and energy on specific initiatives has been worthwhile. What lessons are there for the future?

</td></tr>
</table>

School policies and practices do need to be checked regularly. There is nothing more draining of staff and their motivation than an initiative, which they assumed had taken root, showing signs of withering – either because of neglect, or because it is pushed out by yet another 'initiative'. There needs to be a constant balance between control and creativity and between consolidation and innovation. Without these 'checks and balances' some key staff may start to experience the 'lone-voice' syndrome whereby they imagine they are the only ones keeping to what was agreed.

Another factor in potential 'burn-out' is that both the school calendar and major initiatives tend to generate periods, often quite prolonged, of particularly intense activity. Staff will find the energy to ride these pressure waves, providing they can seek respite in calmer waters from time to time.

Modelling work habits

The most recent research (Goleman 1998a) into 'the best heads and deputies' identified their 'huge' amounts of energy for, and their 'relentless' focus on, raising standards. Coincidentally, they identified the fact that the 'very best **new** heads are doing as well as the best **established** heads'. There are messages here for how the discharge of responsibility is modelled. Staff expect their leaders to be totally committed and to work hard. They look to them as role models. However, there is clearly a limit to how long headteachers and senior managers can continue to expend 'huge amounts' of energy. Overall, the modelling of 'workaholism' by headteachers and team leaders will be counterproductive. Running schools requires all the time staff can give, but working excessively long hours is likely to damage health and harm relationships.

Challenging marginal performance

> 'It is easy to govern a kingdom but difficult to rule one's family.'

Ancient proverb

For a school to be able to operate at peak performance it is essential that 'marginal performance' is regarded as unacceptable. Such a stance needs to be part of the school culture. It needs to be sustained through constant attention from senior managers. For example, a teacher arriving and leaving 'on the dot' each day (or slightly after and slightly before!) must not 'get away with it'. If they do, the culture is quickly undermined. And reprimands, when they come, although not administered publicly, need to be 'seen to happen'. (Unlike a headteacher on a training programme in 2000 who, on getting feedback on staff perceptions of her performance, was surprised to find that staff did not feel she held them accountable. 'But I always have a word', she protested. Unfortunately, it transpired that the 'word' was so discreet as to fail to register with the rest of the staff. To them it was as if the reprimand had never taken place.)

So what is marginal performance?

Marginal performance is not bad enough for capability procedures – but it only just stays above that level. In general, marginal performers offer the minimum of some or all of the following:

◆ hours (below any measure of 1,265 hours);
◆ effort;
◆ overt commitment;
◆ additional voluntary contributions to school life.

The kind of behaviours marginal performers exhibit may include:

◆ going to the pub on a Friday lunchtime and failing the afternoon breath-test;
◆ denigrating pupils in front of colleagues;
◆ insisting, by covert means, on a reserved chair in the staffroom;

- sighing a lot;
- expressing overtly negative views of the school;
- being cynical (poisonous, as in cyanide!);
- taking time off on a regular basis (e.g. odd days here and there);
- focusing on staff social events (excellent but not at the expense of commitment to students);
- not meeting administrative and other deadlines;
- not preparing lessons;
- not marking properly;
- writing brief and often meaningless reports;
- inconsistency with regard to student management (lax on some issues/completely inflexible on others – e.g. insisting on precise sanctions for every offence and then dealing with incidents in her/his own way; responding to students erratically – from overt favouritism to outright hostility);
- claiming loud and long to have 'seen it all before';
- reacting badly to failed job applications (internal or external).

Who are the marginal performers?

The characteristics outlined serve to point up individuals who qualify. However, it is dangerous to stereotype. It is certainly not just an age or 'length of service' condition. Someone approaching retirement, a long-standing member of the staff bridge club, a long-serving caretaker may all sustain high degrees of professional enthusiasm and continue to make positive contributions to the life and work of the school. Conversely, some younger members of staff may drift swiftly into marginal performance, unless their initial commitment is acknowledged and nurtured.

Though the caveat about stereotyping needs to be kept in mind, those members of staff who have been subject to poor role models tend to become marginal performers. This trend is more likely to be confirmed if the staff concerned do not appreciate that the 'professionalism' offered to them was inadequate and if they cannot change their established pattern of behaviour. This risk highlights the need for all school managers to reflect good professional practice, while dealing promptly with any aspects of poor performance.

Certainly, marginal performers must not be confused with 'non-conformists' who give 110% of effort but who don't necessarily follow school procedures. Sometimes it is staff working in creative areas of the curriculum who are non-conformist. The head of art who encourages hours of homework to the detriment of other curriculum areas but whose students' work around the school makes everyone proud; or the drama teacher who throws atypical 'wobblies' around every school production but who always seems to extract stunning performances from the students. From time to time, such non-conformity will have to be addressed in the interests of fairness and consistency, but the approach will be different to that which challenges marginal performance. With the 'effective' non-conformists there is scope to mix sternness and stricture with smiles and praise.

What is the impact of marginal performers on the rest of the school?

The impact of marginal performers will depend, in part, on the status and power they have within the school. An underperforming member of the leadership group or wider management team will clearly impact on a large number of staff at various times, as well as having many opportunities to undermine the head or senior colleagues. In particular, if entrenched attitudes are causing a senior colleague to underperform, the negative consequences can permeate everyone's morale. Like a grammar school deputy who, finding himself in a school reorganisation, took every opportunity to denigrate the comprehensive intake; in particular, the daily pre-school meeting of senior managers started with a debilitating hark-back to a golden yesteryear. The head of department who is under performing will not only undermine the effectiveness of her/his colleagues but will have a damaging effect on the pupils.

In general, the greatest damage inflicted by marginal performers is their demotivating influence on hard-working and committed staff. If the marginal performer 'gets away with it', then damaging questions will be exchanged surreptitiously between staff: Why is X still here? What is going to be done about Y? This is because the school community as a whole sees marginal performers as passengers at best and parasites at worst. Over time, they may reduce that pool of commitment on whose goodwill the schools relies. Increasingly, schools depend on individuals offering what McCormack (1990) calls the 110% solution. Each individual who deliberately operates at 50% or 75% puts an enormous **extra burden** on their colleagues.

Why are they like this?

Research by Goleman (1998a) identified 'understanding others' as a key requirement of effective leadership. Certainly appreciating the 'motives' of colleagues and self can be part of responding appropriately to staff potential and can be helpful in seeking solutions to people-problems (Honey 1980; McClelland 1987; Cava 1990).

However, the possible reasons for underperformance may be legion. They could include one or more of the following:

- current knowledge and skills being insufficient for the task and context, leading to feelings of incompetence;
- frustration because career seems to be at a halt;
- high achievement drive not being satisfied;
- feeling that they have no influence in the 'power stakes';
- failing to reflect on their work and having limited insight and self-awareness;
- having diminished confidence;
- not being in the right role, department or school ('horses for courses');
- wanting an easy life;
- having more engrossing, external interests;
- being in the wrong job;
- feeling hard done by in life;
- family or relationships problems overriding professional interests and actions.

The top half of the list is easier to work with than the bottom half, but all shortcomings require a two-way transaction if there is to be any chance of resolving marginal performance.

Sometimes it just happens by accident, or intuition, and you find you've unlocked great reserves of untapped energy, purpose and productivity in the other person. Too often a variety of approaches may be unproductive, yielding only frustration. However, if disciplinary action or dismissal are unfair or are not options, the only other course of action is to keep trying to change perceptions and responsiveness. Without becoming involved in pseudo-therapy, some possibilities are listed below.

What actions can be taken?

First, try applying McGregor's (1960) Theory X and Theory Y approach to **yourself**. What do you believe motivates your colleagues to perform at the highest level? Are you a Theory X manager, believing that your staff need to be persuaded, rewarded, punished, directed and controlled in order to produce? Or do you work on the Theory Y assumption that people are intrinsically self-motivating and that they possess the capacity to assume responsibility and the potential for development? Your approach to staff and to management problems will almost certainly mirror the way in which you regard the power relationship with students. You may argue that you adopt X and Y approaches according to circumstance, but an underlying bias towards one or the other may have significant implications for the way you operate as leader. Leadership is certainly an area where 'know thyself' and 'compensate for thy weaker reactions' pays off.

Second, ensure you develop the widest possible range of leadership styles and use those colleagues who may be able to utilise a style you find more difficult to sustain. For example, performance management gives the leadership group as a whole the opportunity to promote the **coaching style** through using the 'professional development review structure'. This may enable your marginal performers to be spoken to within a climate of enhanced expectation for all, thus making them feel less vulnerable or exposed. This is because the general focus of performance management is to accept that there are areas of the school that need improving; by means of development targets everyone is looking at their contribution in order to secure that improvement.

Third, although it is unlikely you can change personality, you can change performance. As with students, it is important to believe that marginal performers **want** to achieve, and to remember that 'learning will only take place when the learner wants to learn' (Boyatzis 2000). This means paying attention to ways of getting an individual's true responsiveness to achievement out in the open and matching school opportunities with their readiness to learn. Thus, as with students, some staff may respond to:

◆ short-term targets with dates so that they can more readily see steps in achievement;
◆ an element of pace-setting;
◆ a more direct expression of responsibility;
◆ a stronger say in how things are done;

- peer review – perhaps openness and directness through the adoption of a 'critical friend' who is able to give a 'hard message' but within a supportive atmosphere and framework;
- opportunities to talk through inappropriate behaviour;
- more use of the 'democratic style' of leadership at all levels of school management.

Teachers continue to identify 'insufficient control over the working environment' as a major cause of stress (TES 2000). Though some of this feeling of lack of control lies outside the hands of the leadership group, how far the school exploits all possible facets of shared decision-making will directly contribute to the extent to which individuals feel part of the school 'collective'.

What about sanctions?

You need to decide how troublesome the individuals you are dealing with are. What will be the costs and benefits of taking them on? Will you be able to win any confrontation? Will the adoption of a **coercive style** produce the desired result? There will be 'hidden' costs and benefits of taking action (see Chapter 3). Having weighed up the possible consequences it may be that 'no action' is the best action. Equally, it may be necessary to temporarily live with what you can't change at this particular moment.

Timing of actions is crucial. An early intervention may backfire. You may find that the object of your intervention was about to volunteer to offer a more productive response. On the other hand, there are plenty of schools where nettles grow freely because no one ever grasps them. Not only will they throttle the plants you are trying to encourage, they will also be seen as an ugly and unnecessary eyesore by other staff.

Whatever systems are put in place they must be consistent and be backed up by rigorous evidence arising from classroom observation and, where necessary, careful logging of any breaches of explained and agreed protocol. Staff must be fully aware of:

- line-management arrangements;
- the implications of school policies;
- the general expectations the school has *vis-à-vis* accountability.

Discussion of and agreement on these structures develops a sense of ownership but also indicates criteria by which there can be comeback on those who fail to fulfil their responsibilities

Although your marginal performers must be dealt with, and be seen to be dealt with, there is always the danger that the rest of the staff will feel neglected – analogous to students feeling ignored when one of their peers is put on some type of support programme. The danger is equally great at the other end of the spectrum: constant pandering to peak performers may leave the rest of the staff feeling unable to 'keep up'.

At both ends of the spectrum it is important to emphasise fairness for all staff and consistent staff management and to reinforce these emphases at every opportunity. General points to remember are:

◆ treat all members of staff as individuals;
◆ avoid typecasting and stereotyping;
◆ give clear messages about what is expected in terms of staff responsiveness to school procedures, school routines and the management of student support and student behaviour;
◆ don't label 'subordinates' as 'aggressive', 'bright but awkward', etc. – it supports any trend to label students and if you get it wrong it can be libellous;
◆ practice the use of exploratory questions – When did this begin? What seems to be your difficulty in meeting . . . ? and supportive questions – How can I help get this obstacle removed . . . ? (see Cava 1990 for further advice);
◆ give genuine compliments for real efforts made to improve, (don't make compliments very general – tie them to specific productive reactions);
◆ finally, if you do have to go down the formal procedures road, ensure you have factual data to back up reservations or complaints about performance:

  ◆ analyse staff attendance and punctuality;
  ◆ carry out formalised lesson observations across the school;
  ◆ make notes about any inappropriate responses to self, other colleagues, students, parents and governors – keep these in date order because that demonstrates an organised response and the sequence may indicate a pattern;
  ◆ list failure to meet important deadlines and any excuses given;

◆ in particular, note any 'prejudicial behaviour' in relation to gender, ethnicity, disability, social class background, etc.;

◆ but, on every occasion possible, make it clear that it is the professional performance that is unacceptable, not the person.

Strategic PIN down – Reflection 6.4

Aims

◆ to be able to identify marginal performers;

◆ to employ strategies for dealing with such performance.

P – State the PROBLEM	Marginal performers reduce the effectiveness of the school as a whole. If they are around for a very long time the consequences . . .
I – Clarify the ISSUE	To minimise the effects of underperforming staff we . . .
N – Tackle the NEED	Strategies that help to identify and deal with marginal performance can be grouped as follows . . .

Before you begin, think about:

◆ times when your own performance might have been at the 'margins' or risked being so;

◆ marginal performers you have identified;

◆ marginal performers you have succeeded with;

◆ marginal performers you have failed with;

◆ staff who have been performing at the margins for more than a year;

◆ marginal performers you should be dealing with now.

Tip

Write down some of the leadership qualities and styles you have employed, or seen employed, in dealing successfully with marginal performance.

Interesting facts 4   Personality and performance

In day-to-day conversations we often make a tight connection between personality and performance. We remark, 'they have just the right personality for the job' or 'their personality should enable them to get on with us and make an impression' or 'they've got that "cutting-edge" personality we need'. Are these correct interpretations of personality? And is there a close link between personality traits and job performance? The short answer to both questions is: 'The jury is still out.'

◆ In general, personality is a field of study rather than a particular aspect of people. Social scientists (and many other professionals and lay people) increasingly recognise that complex behaviour has many determinants. Current personality research identifies five key dimensions of personality – neuroticism, extraversion, openness to new experience, agreeableness and conscientiousness (Mischel 1999).

◆ Prediction of job success using personality testing is proving extremely difficult. This is particularly so where, as with teaching, success in the job is multidimensional. In such circumstances, it is not easy to link personality evidence with job-specific success criteria (Kline 1993).

◆ Likewise, complex behaviours that may enter the workplace or influence job responsiveness – such as mild criminality, prejudice against women or others, temperamental tendency to conflagration, etc. – are not unitary concepts that can be matched in one-to-one correspondence with traits such as extraversion/introversion, etc.

◆ Nor is it easy to draw exact parallels or tight links between 'peak performance' and loose descriptions of personality, such as amiable and compliant, analytical and decisive, creative and friendly, a 'mover and shaker', etc.

◆ However, it may be helpful to identify behavioural predispositions in self and others that might help to successfully motivate and manage people, i.e. to become aware of the possible power and pitfalls of personal style with regard to managing for peak performance (Weiss 1989).

Summary

◆ Peak performance essentially describes the best commitment to learning shown by staff and students, and the inextricable link with high academic and professional standards.

◆ Sustaining peak performance depends on attention to both best practice and that which needs improvement.

◆ School effectiveness is more than administrative efficiency. Effectiveness goes beyond meeting basic functional requirements and narrow academic standards. Effective schools pay strong attention to the quality of the educational journey.

◆ To maintain peak performance requires the school leadership to strike a balance between control and creativity.

◆ Knowledge of written descriptions of effective professional practice, leadership styles and theories of motivation can help professional leaders to make sensible decisions along the 'pull–push' continuum.

◆ Responding to marginal performance is as important for school effectiveness, as is the recognition of best professionalism. Marginal performance has to be considered in terms of strategies that may ameliorate it and sanctions that may have to be applied if the inadequate performance remains entrenched.

◆ Knowing staff well helps with all aspects of performance management. It may be useful to examine the behavioural predispositions of one's own approach to management so as to be aware of the possible power and pitfalls of personal style.

Overview

This chapter starts by examining some of the characteristics common to high-performing teams. Working from the base of defending the need for teams and deciding what usage the term 'team' can be put to, the chapter continues by describing some recent images and 'watchwords' used by successful sports teams. An analogy is drawn between these characteristics and the challenges of team management in schools. The chapter concludes with some consideration of how to establish a teamwork culture and what needs to be done to help team effectiveness.

What is a team?

> 'Coming together is a start.
> Staying together is progress.
> Working together is success.'

Henry Ford

Collins English Dictionary (1993) defines a team as a 'group of people organised to work together' and teamwork as 'the co-operative work done by a team'. Katzenbach and Smith (1993) expand on these definitions:

> 'A team is a small number of people with complementary skills who are committed to a common purpose, performance goals and approach for which they hold themselves mutually accountable.'

The general characteristics of successful teams are well known. In the educational context they include:

◆ a clear understanding of everyone's responsibilities within the team;
◆ defined links with other teams;
◆ a common purpose in respect of development planning, the analysis of attainment and the use of staff expertise and resources;
◆ the transfer of knowledge from one to another – e.g. sharing what they know about the craft of teaching and learning;
◆ a collective approach to achieve shared goals;

◆ working together to explore differences and create consensus understanding;

◆ the shaping of a shared educational philosophy and a clear set of values.

Why do we need teams in schools?

Old proverb   'Few burdens are heavy when everyone lifts.'

This question needs answering because in many ways much teaching is still individual working – the bulk of the job being carried out autonomously by teachers in their own classrooms with variable degrees of direction from the top. Indeed, in many European countries and some states of the USA, the idea of a team approach, even at the top of an educational institution, is quite restricted. Leaders are often seen to be chief 'administrators' rather than educational managers, and if there needs to be more than one, that merely reflects a large amount of 'administering' to be done. Many tasks are seen as discrete (for example, budgeting and accounts, testing and examinations, guidance and counselling) and may or may not be carried out by teachers. Although the school's mission may be collectively agreed, there may not be a strong perception of the need to share methods of working – such as planning lessons and managing curricular and departmental responsibilities.

But working in isolation can still be the experience of a teacher at the classroom level in many schools in the UK. Teachers may carry out their prescribed tasks on an individual basis, and recent increased prescriptiveness in the curriculum seems to be leading to a reduction in opportunities for team teaching. Thus, some teachers argue that, with the introduction of the literacy and numeracy hours, the system has moved a step closer to the old French model, by which you could, at one time, set your watch virtually in any part of the country just by looking through a classroom window to see what was being taught.

Certainly there has always been, and most likely will continue to be, tension between the dictates of central prescription – which is sometimes presented as though teachers were just 'instrumental messengers' – and the ever-increasing need for staff in schools to work together to confirm and communicate their own sense of purpose and to meet the demands of more challenging students, more complex professional tasks and more variable working environments.

The origins of teamworking in education are various, but co-operative work received a powerful thrust with the development of the tripartite secondary system. In the first half of the 20th century the grammar and public school 'instructional and tutorial' culture was predominant, with the master seen as a relatively autonomous professional. The main aspects of 'team work' for students and staff were through sport on the playing field. With the exception of one or two schools and some radical educational thinkers, this culture presided throughout schooling until the revisions of the 1944 Education Act. The secondary modern schools of the 1940s and 1950s, along with some of the early comprehensive schools, were freer than hitherto to experiment with curriculum, teaching and teacher deployment.

The raising of the school leaving age (ROSLA) to 16 increased opportunities for some pupils but left many 'waiting for the oddity of secondary education to be over'. Given the reluctance of many 15-year-olds in secondary modern schools to face another year of secondary schooling, many teachers faced sharp challenges to which there were no easy solutions. Blishen provides a clear description of the trials of a new teacher in an inner-London secondary modern school grappling with noise, violence and sheer bloody-minded defiance. Not for this teacher the comfortable fire in the staff common room and the thriving 'old boys' society ready, at the drop of a hat, to raise funds for some worthy cause. However, ROSLA obstacles brought many teachers together, both to share ideas and materials and to develop new courses and new methods of teaching. They began to benefit from informal talking about their work and later from collective activities organised by the teaching unions and the subject associations. What started to be appreciated in this period is now a truism:

Blishen 1969, p. 12

> 'teachers need interaction with, and support from others to avoid becoming exhausted. All teachers need to inspire each other through collaborative work, to take advantage of the power of emotional resources, and to provide the interpersonal safety nets when the going gets rough.'

Hargreaves and Fullan 1998

It is the team qualities of support, cohesion and unity that sustain teachers and prevent them from feeling lonely, neglected and overwhelmed. It is often through very good teamwork that many teachers become most effective. What is vital, however, is that teamwork does not become an end in itself. It is not uncommon in schools for teams to start with a clear professional focus but to drift into largely 'social mode'. That is, the team is happy to give time to meeting together, but the original purpose is lost and the event is little more than an opportunity to 'talk shop'.

Equally, though the affliative leadership style helps team endeavour, since it models positive relationships and harmony, it must not be used inappropriately to sustain teamworking that may need to be surrendered. For example, if a senior and well-liked member of staff is taking time off work and increasingly appearing unable to cope, the natural instinct of the senior management team or a sector team may be to support her/him excessively, particularly if this appears to be what the whole staff want. However, this perception and the circumstances may change in the long term and become counter-productive. The risk is the maintenance of an individual and old team structure, leading to too much of the school's approach becoming that of supporting staff rather than educating children.

What is the best size of a team?

Renault car
advertisement

'Size matters!'

Because there is no single, complete definition of a team, the size of teams in practice varies considerably. The size will vary with regard to:

◆ the purpose of the team;
◆ the availability of people who can make up a suitable group;
◆ the urgency for a decision or action;
◆ the nature of the endeavour the team has to undertake;
◆ the scope for sharing the action – i.e. necessarily confined to a few staff, versus the opportunity to involve all who wish to volunteer.

Whilst half-a-dozen may be a practical size for regular interaction, the notion of 'the team' can be applied to include everyone who works or supports an organisation. For example, Sir Richard Branson (the head of the Virgin group) regularly refers to the thousands of workers in Virgin as 'my team'; Sir John Egan, the chief executive of BAA spoke in an interview of the need to get 'large groups of people to work in harmony with each Egan 1998 other to a common purpose'; politicians often speak about the 'party as a working team'; and football managers speak with passion about the supporters who are the 'real team behind the team'. Thus a team may be created from any of the natural operational units within an organisation, or it can be the image, wide collegiality or vast collaboration that represents the identified ethos of a multinational company or world-stage sports team.

Though the context of the organisation and the focus of the task will often determine the purpose of the team and its practical size, some issues in any organisation do need to be put to everyone, and there has to be a wide period of consultation across the board before key decisions or key objectives are arrived at.

Strategic PIN down – Reflection 7.1

Aim

◆ to ensure the widest possible participation in policy-making where the issues under consideration relate to the whole school and implementation involves all staff.

P – State the PROBLEM — If staff do not have 'ownership' of school policies their implementation will be adversely affected because . . .

I – Clarify the ISSUE — Understanding how strategic decision-making occurs is critical to ensuring . . .

N – Tackle the NEED — Therefore, to identify actual and ideals levels of participation in decision-making should help to . . .

Before you begin, think about:

◆ Who will be responsible for carrying out a suitable survey or action-based research exercise?

◆ Will **all** staff be asked their views?

◆ What will be the process for analysing staff feedback? Who will do it?

◆ How will wider involvement in policy-making benefit from the exercise?

Tip

Be careful not to raise expectations until you have some firm evidence that there actually is a need to increase participation.

Teamwork generates commitment

> 'The inevitable end of multiple chiefs is that they fade and disappear for lack of unity.'
>
> Napoleon Bonaparte

The use of the terms 'team' and 'teamwork' not only reflect the way in which an organisation is run; the words themselves have the potential to generate commitment. However, to do so means breaking away from long-established working practices that may compartmentalise thinking and the way staff work. It means introducing structures where decision-making is close to those who have to carry out the implementation, and reducing as far as is feasible line-management or communication arrangements that are excessively hierarchical or that intersperse long periods of time between referral and decision. It also means ensuring that there is a healthy respect for all viewpoints. Effective schools usually have these features in place. They have developed a real understanding of a shared culture of achievement to a point where all staff are involved in the life and work of the school, not just the teachers. The recognition that the catering staff, bursar and cleaners, as much as the heads of departments, have a vital role to play, generates a 'big team' approach that can do much to promote and protect the school image.

Issues in focus 7.1

There are no certain ways to successfully involve all. However, those who have put the idea into practice suggest that the following constitute important features of large-group harmony:

◆ Involving all is not seen as a 'cause'. It is a practical approach to ensuring that 'all' feel a sense of belonging and commitment.
◆ What 'all involved' means is discussed – so that there is no *laissez-faire* interpretation.
◆ There is appreciation of and respect for all roles and responsibilities.
◆ There is not a deliberate climate of competitiveness.
◆ There is regular refreshment of what people should be doing – to prevent overlap, duplication and possible conflict.
◆ There is an acceptance of the fact that there will be times when one person decides.
◆ The notion of 'all involved' is kept active. There is regular fresh thinking about how to keep everyone on board.

Loyalty to the 'common purpose'

Salome and
Galland

'On a building site, three stone-cutters are hewing stones. Someone passing by asks them what they are doing. The first one answers: "I'm cutting stones." The second answers: "I'm building a wall." The third one says: "I'm building a cathedral." '

No team – large or small – will work effectively without being committed to a common purpose. The best common purpose will be the greater good of the school. This has to be put above the team itself, the issue in question or even the frail ego of the leader.

Notice board 5   Facing flying facts

Owen (2000) describes nine Red Arrows flying wing-tip to wing-tip. This requires total teamwork, to the point where even the most talented pilots are better served giving support to their colleagues rather than showing off their own skills. Her description of the way in which one particular pilot had to be put out of the team because his performance was not suitable is particularly revealing of the extent to which teamwork informed the Red Arrow culture. The leader in this case did not take the decision alone. It was taken by the team as a whole and the leader implemented it. If such an approach can be adopted in the armed forces then it should be possible in schools. Perhaps all it needs is the discarding of some macho posturing.

Interesting facts 5   Sporting images – the British Lions and their 'watchwords'

The word 'team' is closely associated with sport and sporting images. The use of the term in sport can be helpful in understanding the concept in practice elsewhere. For example, good team managers, the role of coaching, a focus on improving a system or set of results, the player-manager, the team and strategy co-ordinator, rule changes and motivating and inspiring – all have their counterparts in leading and managing teams in any organisation. So does the use of 'action statements' and 'watchwords' as mechanisms for uplift and drive.

The British Lions rugby team that toured South Africa in 1997 was one of the most successful in rugby history. A great deal was written about the way they were managed and their cohesion as a team. They had a number of 'watchwords' to help sustain their commitment and focus. Many of these relate directly to teamwork as it applies in schools.

Discipline (self and team)   In the context of rugby, one meaning of discipline is staying sufficiently concentrated to not give away unnecessary penalties. In the context of school teamwork, it can mean remaining focused on the task in hand, not hogging meeting time, remaining loyal to unpalatable decisions and maintaining punctuality.

Belief (self and team)   This means having the confidence to contribute to a team and being able to recognise what others offer and what they might offer. It encompasses the notion that no mountain is too high and everything is possible.

Identity   A mission statement attracting the widest possible ownership is an excellent start towards establishing what the school as a whole stands for. As with sporting images, such statements need to be visible and accessible. They might include references to the principles and assumptions underpinning the school's work, equal opportunities and a code of behaviour. Without donning the uniforms worn by representatives of public companies or corporate bodies, there should be visible and invisible signs of identity and belonging. Some schools use logos and the design and presentation of school facilities to good effect. Others concentrate less on the visible signs but do much to encourage staff cohesion through how the school is described and discussed and how its successes and failures are handled.

Cohesive   When the chips are down, most people will naturally stick and act together. However, the ultimate goal is to ensure that the team comes across as one body on a day-to-day basis. Effective teamwork presents a united voice. It is not a collection of diverse and disparate individuals. Adair (1987) indicates that a:

p. 108

> 'test for a cohesive team is whether or not its members can work as a team while they are **apart**, contributing to a sequence of activities rather than always to a common task which requires their presence in one place and at one time'.

Supportive   A rugby tour, indeed any series of major sporting events involving travel, acclimatisation and different types of representation, will present the team with troughs and peaks, ups and downs. Often these will coincide with the greater or lesser contributions of individuals. In order to sustain harmony and maintain team purpose and spirit, individuals need to help each other out through the thick and the thin, even though this may call for high degrees of self-sacrifice.

Trust   All team members need to feel that they can trust each other with confidences, with responsibilities and with the team's mission. Students who deliberately tell malicious lies are bad enough, but staff who do so can cause significant problems, even irreversible difficulties. Perhaps the beacon of trust in schools centres around workload. Effective teams selflessly contribute for the good of the team overall; they resist the many temptations in the 'hothouse' atmosphere of the school to undermine colleagues or to take advantage of them. They will focus on the 'people needs' end of a challenge, attuning their response so as to maintain the best climate for the students, team and school. Staff need to be aware how much damage even a small minority of untrustworthy malcontents can cause.

Openness and honesty   Good sporting teams are so because, despite the presence of very talented individuals, much of the successful play is concerted action where individuals feed off each other. There is openness and honesty about each individual's potential and their right to be involved, coupled with trust that when mistakes occur they are attributed to the team as a whole, not some chosen scapegoat (even though the media may choose this path). Teamwork in schools is no different. Feeling secure to say what you think is the foundation for making significant contributions. When others see honesty – at the expense of feeling vulnerable and unpopular – they are encouraged to behave likewise. Sadly, in closed systems, the 'I never have/had any problems with that class/parent/senior colleague' continues to persist – undermining both confidence and a collective approach to solutions.

United   A team's game plan is the way in which it tries to prepare for and protect unity and cohesion. All good game plans rest on mutual understanding of what is being proposed and why, a belief in colleagues' best efforts on the day and respect for any modifications to the plan from those in a position to oversee the whole action.

Committed   Commitment is a word that is often overhyped in sporting commentary. Frequently, this is by media and fans, perhaps more than by any team itself. Successful teams often recognise that the level of commitment is the source of many other team qualities. They know that commitment is closely linked to the motivation of individuals who make up the team. Hence the time that is spent in rehearsing the team's identity, seeking ways to maintain a high level of collective response and ensuring that success is stamped with the team's contribution, even when individuals have played an outstanding part.

Flexible   Increasingly, sporting teams have to be flexible. The ever-present risk of significant injury, the more open use of substitutes, the rapidly changing nature of a team's fortunes and the denationalisation of some sporting boundaries mean that changing team membership, revised strategies and a tireless pursuit for success require individuals to be maximally responsive. Flexibility of this kind is similar in the ever-changing world of education. Staff at all levels have to be alert to the potential offered by new initiatives and new challenges. Teams, if they are to be effective, will need to grapple with change and be able to shed outdated or outmoded attitudes and opinions.

Punctuality   In rugby and other sporting events, it is no use not making the start time or the start line. It is not helpful to colleagues to be off the pace and out of reach of the pass. It is no good getting ready to join in an action when the time for it has passed. Punctuality and attention to task, or the lack of them, mark out the culture of an organisation. It is useful for all teams to explore openly the significance of being on time and meeting deadlines. Such focus will inevitably act as a stimulus for discussing the underpinning characteristics of commitment, consideration and respect.

No cliques   A scrum, a rowing eight, a dance formation team, a volley ball squad all need to function as single entities without cliques. The action has to be orchestrated across the team as a whole. Also, the harmony developed through training has to be sustained when the going gets tough. Similarly, co-ordination of drive, action and effort has to be achieved in all organisations if work is to be cohesive and purposeful. In reality, cliques tend to reflect a **lack** of teamwork. Where there is genuine common purpose and shared commitment across the **whole** staff, then the need for cliques, with their secure defences, will be diminished.

Sensitivity   In the context of muscle-bound six-foot-two rugby players, 'sensitivity' might seem out of place. However, the ability to 'take the role of the other', to empathise with colleagues' aspirations and disappointments, to get inside the heads and hearts of colleagues so as to work productively with them, and to see alternate courses of action depends on being sensitive to one's own feelings and those of others.

Strategic PIN down – Reflection 7.2

Aim

◆ to establish a school environment where there are no exclusive staff cliques.

P – State the PROBLEM

New staff can find it difficult to settle in. Where the staff room is not an inviting place for teaching staff, non-teaching staff, old or new staff it will be necessary to . . .

I – Clarify the ISSUE

To ensure that teamwork and a 'whole school' sense of purpose become hallmarks of our effectiveness we . . .

N – Tackle the NEED

Where separate groups or cliques within the staff occur, initial steps towards closer work as a whole staff might be . . .

Before you begin, think about:

◆ the impact, positive and negative, of individuals;
◆ the times and circumstances where staff work best together;
◆ the extent to which the school's induction programme contributes to staff integration.

Tip

Do not try to shift the focus of the school from professional to social; concentrate on work-based strategies likely to lead to greater interaction.

One of the main differences between commercial sporting teams and those in schools is, of course, the fact that the principal aim of a funded sporting team is to 'win'. This means firm action in the areas of team selection, dropping underperforming players, putting individuals on the transfer list and, where funds permit, buying 'superstars'. No doubt many a headteacher has engaged in the fantasy of operating these powerful actions. However, not all success is bankrolled.

Lessons from football – Brian Clough and Kevin Keegan

> 'You must first be a believer if you wish to be an achiever.'

Anonymous

In football circles it is often said that to achieve a winning team today requires the support of a rich sponsor or a patient bank manager. This may be so, but even the best achievers slip from time to time, and there are plenty of teams around to demonstrate that consistent winning is a lot more than simply buying the best.

Replays from the past also demonstrate this fact. For example, the Nottingham Forest teams that Brian Clough put together in the 1970s won two European Cups with players costing only a fraction of those in other top clubs. All this was done through the generation of stunning teamwork, based on qualities matching those of the Lions some twenty years later.

Footballing *cognoscenti* will be quick to point out that Clough was a martinet who managed through a rule of fear and patronage. In this way he reflected an approach to management that became the norm during the Thatcher years and has lasted right through into the 21st century. Although many successful managers established much more democratic regimes, there is a danger that the success of the Clough approach might be seen as the simple answer to the complex challenge of running a school.

Kevin Keegan, like Clough, was clearly able to motivate his players, but some commentators consider he never learnt to 'boss' them in the way that Clough did. They both take some comfort from McGregor (1960), who gave us Theory X and Theory Y. McGregor said that he thought he:

> 'could avoid being a "boss" . . . I thought that maybe I could operate so that everyone would like me – that "good human relations" would eliminate all discord and disagreement. I couldn't have been more wrong. It took a couple of years, but I finally began to realise that a leader cannot avoid the exercise of authority any more than he can avoid the responsibility for what happens to his organisation.'

We would not want to argue with the notion that authority has to be exercised or that the leader has to take responsibility for what happens in her/his organisation. However, the autocratic approach adopted by Clough and others would depend much too heavily on the 'coercive' style of leadership (see Chapter 2). Schools recruit staff, offer them permanent contracts and have to make a long-term commitment to them. This is a far cry from the world of football management where buying and selling players and hiring and firing them (and their managers) are the norm.

Overall, managers of sports teams and effective headteachers do need to possess and to demonstrate a range of similar qualities. These include:

- a sense of what the best can be;
- a willingness to build towards it;
- the tenacity to keep going through the toughest of times when despair and failure outweigh triumph and success;
- an approach to bring out the best in those they manage;
- the capacity to praise good performance and act to improve what is below the mark;
- loyalty to the team and those who support them.

However, the difference between the two is that many sports team managers rarely need to put themselves on an equal plane with their players and ground staff, whereas headteachers are required to play a greater variety of roles. This can be the whole gamut from team leader through team member to team junior responding to team requests. Thus, although schools, like some football and other sporting clubs, operate very tight hierarchical systems, school leaders need to be able to operate much more flexibly and with a much stronger focus on sharing both policy and practice.

Hierarchies and the 'fear factor'

> 'A man's style is his mind's voice.'

Ralph Waldo
Emerson

Handy (1976) has contrasted 'organisations which rely on trust as their principal means of control . . . [and] are more effective, more creative, more fun and cheaper to operate' with 'organisations . . . based on hierarchical control systems [and] with an unspoken undercurrent of fear'. Schools are, of course, a cog in the whole hierarchical control system that is the world of education. At the top of the pyramid is the secretary of state for education, responsible for implementing the government's agenda of reforms. Next, are the local education authorities, which, though increasingly emasculated, still have the power to 'frighten' schools (viz. the deference – often quite unwarranted – some schools still show to chief education officers and LEA monitoring systems). Then comes each school's governing body with, at its head, the chair of governors – with whom senior managers have to establish a good working relationship.

With such a hierarchical administrative structure, it is not surprising that efforts can founder at first base – however strong a school's desire to operate a 'team' approach. Extending the metaphor a little, 'first base' can be taken to mean the bottom of the pyramid, where those with the least control and pay reside. These are the staff who when things are failing, are most likely to say: 'You're paid for it. You do it.' Some of these staff increasingly feel that because of the way central reforms have been presented, they have moved further away from creative modes of teaching and towards mechanistic styles of instruction. Heads and LEAs are now seen by some teachers as no more than 'messengers', relaying centralised curriculum, centralised procedures for planning and assessment and centralised 'advice' about teaching that is really dictate in disguise. For their part, some headteachers and LEA officers see themselves being prepared for the firing squad because they are thought to be collaborating with more and more reductions in teacher autonomy and with central moves towards less rather than more professionalism.

Counteracting the 'fear factor' – the power of synergy

Lady Bird Johnson

> 'The way to overcome is to be so wrapped up in something you forget to be afraid.'

Strong teamwork within the microcosm of the individual school and between schools and their partner LEA can counter the negative influence of hierarchical structures. The strength will lie in:

◆ establishing mutually supportive advice and communication systems that integrate common requirements – e.g. the collection, analysis and use of pupil performance and other school data;

◆ making sure that the 'positives' that emerge from day-to-day work receive their fair share of attention and are communicated to all partners – in other words avoiding perceptions that it is all 'top–down' messages about failures;

◆ looking at ways to ensure that central initiatives are meaningfully contextualised for the schools and the local community, and that as far as possible they are used to support local curriculum enhancement;

◆ ensuring an orchestrated approach for teachers, students and parents with regard to their understanding of what is statutory and what is discretionary;

◆ making clear what contributions all 'key players' are making to students' education and welfare.

Effective teams unlock the power of 'synergy', whether within the context of a school or across a broader partnership. That is, the group outperforms its best individual member working alone, and the 'whole becomes greater than the sum of the parts'. Synergy develops momentum and draws people in whereas individual effort and energy can so easily be dissipated.

Example 1: Homework   School A sets homework according to no particular timetable or time allocation. School B has discussed and agreed all aspects of the homework programme before any communication with students or their parents. Although commitment to the value of homework is the same in the two schools, the messages coming across are quite different. In school A, homework set by one department or faculty is seen as a quite different activity, and possibly with different purposes, than that set by another department or faculty. In school B, the messages about homework are consistent and clear to the point where pupils tell new or substitute teachers what they should be setting and when it is due. School B has worked through any inconsistencies and disagreements. They have not established a view too quickly and assumed it will be implemented consistently. They have achieved real consensus and this underpins a 'whole school' response. The whole has become greater than the linking together of the parts.

Example 2: Equal opportunities   School A has agreed that 'all issues of discrimination must be confronted' but staff have not agreed a proper policy or clear procedures. School B has devoted considerable time to a whole staff discussion of the issues, and the discussion has resulted in written outcomes. These have involved students. The written reminders are now accessible and displayed around the premises. As with the homework example above, the results in the two schools are quite different. In school A, the student perception is of a myriad of individual approaches, some of which can seem arbitrary and unfair. In school B, the line is so consistent that, again, students can be heard enforcing the policy themselves.

Goleman (1998a) explores the effects of synergy through what he calls 'Group IQ'. He asks, 'What makes a team perform better than the best person in it?' and concludes that the **relationships** between members are p. 205 key. By this he means the ability to resolve differences, communicate effectively and foster 'internal harmony'. Shared goals play a crucial role, as does motivation generally. The ability of team members to relate to each others' ideas, attitudes and feelings elevates the effectiveness of the team to a high level.

Teams as problem identifiers and problem solvers

> 'A community is like a ship: everyone ought to be prepared to take the helm.'

Henrik Ibsen

Most people seem to believe that teams expand horizons and extend options. Unfortunately, there are still some leaders of schools and organisations who think that all wisdom resides in them. They have nothing to learn from subordinates and need no help to find answers to problems. In contrast, in Chapter 6 we outlined a situation where a leader of a successful multinational company claimed he never needed ideas of his own because his colleagues had so many. Sir John Egan, chief executive of BAA pursues a similar line:

> 'We've delegated authority to people to do the best they can within a very clear management system where they're empowered. I think part of the secret of managing is to manage in a way that appears as though you're not there – that people have done it themselves. . . . When everyone's pulling on the same piece of rope, it does actually look pretty easy – though sometimes it's not.'

Egan 1998

The use of the word 'appears' might raise an eyebrow, but Egan follows this by claiming that 'most of his ideas come from somebody else'. Such respect for teamwork and for the contribution that colleagues can make to the identification and solution of problems goes hand-in-hand with a fully controlled ego. If a headteacher cannot resist the desire to claim the credit for all the school's successes, then the creative help that produces it will quickly dry up. As we have emphasised at various points, teamwork involves 'respect' for others. This includes generous acknowledgement of their contribution.

The irony is that the more a leader can listen to, accept and acknowledge the contribution of others, the more empowered subordinates become. In turn, the organisation tends to be successful, leading to praise for leader from the staff and others.

Modelling teams from the top

> 'People are more apt to follow your lead than the way you point.'

Anonymous

In some schools there is a strong tradition of indifference – or sometimes outright hostility – to senior managers. Both reactions can be justified. The London headteacher who had lines drawn on the floor of her office to indicate her availability (from 'Yes, you can come in' to 'Do not interrupt me unless you really have to') was not encouraging collective decision-making and teamwork. Nor do those traffic light systems outside the doors of headteachers' offices – red for 'Go away' and green for 'Even though my door is closed you may risk coming in'.

The Yorkshire grammar-turned-comprehensive school, where you knew you were in the senior management area because the corridor was full of coat hooks with academic gowns, did little to foster co-operation across a new school staff. The term 'hierarchy boulevard' was used in a Lancashire school to describe a similar situation.

In general, these 'traditions' tend to accentuate divisions between senior managers and the rest of the staff. Though 'by appointment' has to be the case at times, if senior managers are to administer efficiently, staff know only too well when a system is there to block genuine communication or to reinforce the 'I know best' philosophy.

Reducing the effects of these traditions and establishing positive teamwork requires that senior managers expend time and effort on promoting the type of culture embodied in the 'watchwords' discussed earlier. Genuine developments in team activities and benefits will encourage key-stage, departmental, faculty and year teams to do likewise. Actions likely to begin and sustain teamwork will include:

◆ agreeing on processes that encourage as much openness as possible;
◆ always looking for the 'most acceptable' outcome rather than one that assumes 'winners and losers';
◆ the development of systems that help to share the workload;
◆ collectively designing and implementing regular and secure 'links' between different sections of the school;
◆ using structures that don't 'cement in' hierarchical authority – for example, rotating chairs of meetings, using rapporteurs from the staff to observe and report on outcomes from different angles, building cross-representative working parties;
◆ ensuring that the necessary mechanisms of team work are well oiled – for example, agenda and minutes produced in good time, necessary resources to hand;

◆ showing how team decisions have been accepted and acted on;

◆ showing genuine gratitude when everyone has 'mucked in' to retrieve a situation or prevent a disaster;

◆ regularly checking that systems have not locked into minutiae at the expense of 'no one steering the ship and looking after the crew'.

Strategic PIN down – Reflection 7.3	**Aims** ◆ to establish the leadership group as a dynamic and positive team in the school; ◆ to ensure it provides an excellent model for all other staff.

P – State the PROBLEM	There is insufficient time for senior management business, too many meetings overrun or take place unplanned and they often begin with not all members present. To rectify this we need to . . .
I – Clarify the ISSUE	To ensure that colleagues feel they are full and equal members of the SMT at all times – even when they are unable to attend meetings or discussions – we have to . . .
N – Tackle the NEED	To clarify exactly how the SMT operates – including dealing with unanticipated situations that require immediate discussion and action – implies . . .

Before you begin, think about:

◆ whether all members of SMT are treated equally;

◆ ways in which the location of SMT offices is impacting on SMT meetings and work;

◆ the extent to which you can, and want, to treat all members of your SMT equally.

Tip

The more synergy you establish at the top of the organisation, the better the role model for all other staff.

The staff as a team

Gardners' World   'Home grown is always the best.'

We have already referred to the size of teams. Popular description tends to present teams as relatively small units of people coming together either regularly or from time to time to work on specific tasks. However, organisations such as schools, if they are run effectively, will manifest a 'team' culture such as we have already described in connection with Virgin and BAA.

Peters and Waterman (1982), in their study of top American companies, identified numerous examples of such cultures from 'Family Feeling' at Delta to 'The HP Way' at Hewlett-Packard. All the businesses they looked at were characterised by structural features that impacted on workers in a very direct manner and enabled them to feel they were part of organisations that were not only successful but were distinctive in terms of their employment practices. Peters and Waterman constructed what they termed their '7–S Framework' – 'Structure, Systems, Style, Staff, Skills, Strategy' and, at the heart of the model, 'Shared Values'. Through their attention to all these areas – but particularly to the last one – the companies concerned were able to generate genuine corporate loyalty and commitment. Workers throughout these organisations felt they had control over their work, that they were respected and, above all, that they understood the purpose of their efforts.

The best schools will engender in their staff feelings similar to those experienced by workers in the companies studied by Peters and Waterman. They achieve this in a variety of ways: First, there is a shared understanding by staff of how they plan and deliver teaching and learning. Typically this shared understanding extends to democratic decision-making about:

◆ the learning process;
◆ the curriculum structure – so that it is wide and imaginative;
◆ the consistency in writing and using schemes of work and lesson plans;
◆ the use of learning environments in an integrated way;
◆ the students' involvement in the life and work of the school;
◆ the professional development needs;
◆ the finance and resource management;
◆ the priorities in staff recruitment and staff deployment.

Second, every opportunity is taken to disseminate the school culture – to the point where it is absorbed not only by staff but by students, parents and the local community. Third, successes are always publicised to the widest possible audience helping to develop powerful and positive self-fulfilling prophecies. Fourth, problems (whatever their source) are dealt with speedily and with determination. The result is deep-rooted pride and identification within the institution about the institution. The only enemy then is complacency.

Types of teams

Old English saying

> 'There are two reasons why we don't trust people: one, because we don't know them; and the other, because we do.'

Organisational and task – formal and informal

Any institution is full of teams, whether they are described as such or not. They all interact and all see themselves as part of a greater whole. However, two main types of team can be identified. First, 'organisational' teams. These are part of the ongoing life of the school and include the senior management team, department/faculty teams, year teams, key-stage teams, learning support teams, pastoral teams. These are teams whose meetings can, and should, be planned well in advance and whose work needs to be kept under constant review. It is very easy for these teams to slip into ways of working that are not necessarily productive – e.g. SMTs where the head always produces the agenda (often on the day of the meeting), always chairs the meetings her/himself and never finds time for anything other than day-to-day business. In fact, because of the structure of the school calendar, such meetings can productively be planned during the summer term for the following year. Such planning should also take account, not only of the calendar, but also of the school development plan.

The other main type of team is a 'task' team set up to deal with particular issues, for example, achievements of boys, school journeys, staff development activities, equal opportunities issues. This type of team usually has a limited life. However, they provide excellent opportunities not only for staff collaboration, and therefore ownership of the outcome, but also for individual development.

Both types of teams are likely to operate at formal and informal levels, that is, individual members of the teams will meet outside of formal meetings. It is important that these informal exchanges are handled carefully, otherwise other members of the team may start to feel left out.

This is particularly true of the school's main, and most active, team – the Senior Management Team.

The Senior Management Team

With the changes resulting from performance management introduced in 2000, most schools will have absorbed those on the leadership group into their SMT. Certainly, with the responsibilities expected of this group it would be incongruous were they not members of the SMT.

Some headteachers have traditionally run a kind of 'inner' (or 'kitchen') cabinet so that SMT meetings operate on two levels – one being the full SMT, the other being the head and her/his deput(y)ies. This may be convenient, in that the head and deputies will have more non-contact time and therefore be more available for meetings. However, in terms of generating senior management ownership of policies and practice, such a structure can be divisive.

There are similar dangers with informal meetings between the headteacher and senior management colleagues. It may well be that the matter is urgent and X is teaching whilst Y and Z are available. In such circumstances, it is essential to brief X at the earliest possible opportunity. One way of facilitating such informal meetings is to locate SMT offices near the heart of the school. The downside of such a practice is the loss of informal supervision in what may be relatively isolated and vulnerable parts of the school (for example, those areas where there is a risk of a variety of student misbehaviour). Prioritising the latter over the former may mean sacrificing the long term for the short term.

One secondary head (whose school eventually went into special measures) managed to get everything wrong when he located his own office in a new purpose-built administration block (see pp. 94–5). He saw neither pupils nor senior managers – except by appointment. Neither did they see him – except by appointment.

Ideally, the SMT should be as large as possible, commensurate with budget constraints and with the need to work effectively. One way in which a number of schools get round budget constraints limiting the size of their leadership groups is by taking middle managers on to their SMT for limited periods of time – say two middle managers for a term and then another two and so on (see Chapter 8). The advantages of such an arrangement are considerable:

◆ Middle managers are given some excellent training.
◆ The arena for thinking through issues and coming up with solutions is widened.
◆ Links between the headteacher and the rest of staff are widened.
◆ Though costs will depend on whether SMT meetings are held in or out of school, they will, at worst, involve some periods of cover.

Strategic PIN down – Reflection 7.4

Aims

◆ to expand contributions from senior staff to the senior management team;
◆ to provide training for middle managers;
◆ to provide better links between the SMT and the rest of staff.

P – State the PROBLEM	The SMT is too small and too remote from the rest of staff. The action we need to take is . . .
I – Clarify the ISSUE	In general, decision- and policy-making should be spread more widely. We plan to . . .
N – Tackle the NEED	Involving middle managers in the work of the SMT without significantly increasing running costs means . . .

Before you begin, think about:

◆ what the optimum size is for the SMT in your school (including additional staff);
◆ how long you want additional staff to be on the SMT for;
◆ whether there are any issues of confidentiality and how these will be handled;
◆ how much you can afford to spend on bringing in extra staff for meetings;
◆ what may be alternative ways of operating the SMT, so that meeting time is reduced.

Tip

There are pluses (e.g. increasing staff involvement) and minuses (e.g. working with staff who would not normally be considered SMT material) but the pluses far outweigh the minuses. So think this exercise through.

How teams operate

> 'Work in meetings is like a soft chair – easy to get into but hard to get out of.'
>
> Anonymous

As with all aspects of school management the 'what' will operate effectively only if attention is paid to the 'how'. There follows some suggestions for 'team maintenance' through formal meetings and by other means.

Formal meetings

Attendance   Make sure members can attend. A casual approach to dates and times may well generate unnecessary paranoia on the part of staff who can't be there.

Minutes   Ensure that those new to minuting know what they should be reporting – i.e. not everything that was said nor even a summarised discussion. Minutes should contain decisions and action points. Most importantly, those individuals responsible for the implementation of action must be identified – with a deadline by which the action must be in place.

Chairing for positive outcomes

◆ Publish agendas as far in advance as possible.
◆ Where there are no papers, indicate the nature of agenda items and, if possible, whether they are for decision or discussion.
◆ Allocate times for each item under discussion and, while retaining flexibility, try not to overrun them.
◆ Start on time.
◆ Don't allow external interruptions – especially resist the temptation to be called out yourself. Many staff will interpret such behaviour as 'puffed-up' and 'self-important' or as a scaling down of the importance of the team (emergencies/disasters excepted, of course).
◆ Ensure minutes are being taken.
◆ Encourage participation by all group members.
◆ Try to talk as little as possible and remain neutral.
◆ Don't overrun the finish time.
◆ Suggest, or make, seating changes if necessary. Eye contact can certainly influence the atmosphere – whether it's friendly or hostile.

◆ Talk to individuals privately to deal with conflict or inappropriate behaviour.
◆ Check minutes for accuracy and brevity.

Issues in focus 7.2

Bell (1990) gives additional good advice about how to sustain teamwork in business meetings, and Everhard and Morris (1996) provide a set of questions designed to ensure that meetings are purposeful – and hence likely to sustain and not disintegrate the team. Their questions (adapted) are:

◆ Is the purpose of the meeting clear to those who attend?
◆ Is the membership correct for the issues under consideration?
◆ Are the participants adequately prepared for the meeting?
◆ Is time well used?
◆ Are there sufficient strategies in use to encourage participation?
◆ Is a clear direction being given on:

  ◆ actions to be taken?
  ◆ criteria to judge the success of the actions?
  ◆ mechanisms to review the action?

◆ Does the commitment/motivation of the group need attention?

General team maintenance

There are many other means of engaging colleagues in productive teamwork, but like meetings they need regular review to ensure that the team's purpose, spirit, focus and productivity are maintained.

Team learning occurs when a group get together to 'learn together' some aspect of planning or practice. They usually then cascade this to others. The focus of the learning could be strategic (e.g. techniques for whole school planning), technological (e.g. use of information and communication technology (ICT) for data collection and analysis), pedagogical (how to extend reading development skills across the curriculum) or evaluative (how to set up, implement and evaluate a scheme of school self-review). For a group to become a 'learning team' implies a good match between the experience on offer and the professional needs. If some colleagues are to train others, the learning will also need to model good process and suitable training techniques.

Working groups Many schools have working groups to provide a suitable impetus to some general development need or to meet a post-inspection requirement. They may work informally or use brainstorming, survey and action-research techniques. Team maintenance is usually enhanced by clear purpose, a sufficient mix of convergent and divergent thinkers, fair representation across the staff and genuine interest in the task on the part of the SMT.

Organisational or role-related teams These types of teams may be subject-based, provision-based (for example, support teams to develop provision to meet special educational needs), research-based or cross-curricular. Their purpose, mode of working, messages and general demeanour need to be congruent with the SMT, the school's mission statement and the school's development plan.

Since most staff will belong to more than one team, senior managers need to put aside time, perhaps on a term basis, to check the development of all the school's teams. In so doing, they may need to check each team's state of development against what is known to happen in teams in general. Field *et al*. (2000) consider four stages of general team development – 'Forming, Storming, Norming and Performing' – and these are discussed in more detail in the first book in this series (McCall and Lawlor 2000). They also need to check that team membership is spread as widely as possible and that it does not operate on the basis of 'if you want a job done find a busy person'. Such practices should help avoid the danger of burn-out described in Chapter 6.

Finally, remember that a headteacher does not have to do all of the jobs. In the long term, the more you can let go and empower your staff, the better it is for the school.

Strategic PIN down – Reflection 7.5	Aims
	◆ to organise the running of the SMT meeting so that all members feel they know what items are to be discussed;
	◆ to ensure all have a significant input into the process.

P – State the PROBLEM	Meetings can appear badly planned; they overrun and are dominated by short-term, day-to-day matters. This can be avoided if . . .
I – Clarify the ISSUE	'The SMT should be planning ahead throughout the year – not just reacting to whatever comes up.' We prevent/deal with this criticism by . . .
N – Tackle the NEED	To draft and agree agendas and to prepare well in advance for meetings requires . . .

Before you begin, think about:

◆ what items you know you will have to discuss at more or less the same time each term, e.g. options, open evening(s);

◆ what distinction, in terms of time, to make between short-term and long-term developments;

◆ how you will monitor and evaluate any changes.

Tip

In running your SMT meetings, there will always need to be a balance, between structure and flexibility.

Is teamwork the same as collegiality ?

Sign on a church board

> 'We cannot all play the same instrument, but we can all be in the same key.'

Collegiality, as it is currently understood, includes teamwork – but, in practice, the terms are synonymous. Where staff work effectively as a team a high degree of collegiality will be present – for example, an environment where sharing is the norm, where discussion and debate are open and where there is a recognition that the whole is greater than the sum of the parts. Of course, with the use of electronic mail, computer conferencing and video conferencing growing at a pace, collegiality may have to take on a broader meaning. Today it is possible for teams and team members to cross national boundaries, co-ordinate discussion within and outside normal timetables, and make links across widespread and even remote geographical areas. The main school team may indeed have a 'whole world' as well as 'whole school' focus.

Summary

'Great minds have purposes; others have wishes.'

Old proverb

◆ Teams may have generic or specific objectives. As staff can belong to more than one team, both individuals and teams need to know what they are accountable for.

◆ The strength of teamwork varies from school to school. The most effective teams have similar characteristics, including a belief that they can achieve more worthwhile outcomes by working together than by working as isolated individuals. Being 'greater than the sum of the parts' is the core benefit from teamworking for teachers.

◆ The best sporting images and watchwords reflect important qualities of good teams. They can be used for both team development and team review.

◆ The size and make-up of teams will vary according to their function and task. For identity, promotion, motivation, marketing and collegiality purposes, whole organisations are sometimes legitimately analysed as 'teams'.

◆ Explicit and shared values are necessary to sustain teams. Effective teamwork also depends on efficient structures to meet and work together.

◆ Strong collegiality underpins harmonious and constructive teamwork. In the light of ICT-based links, teamwork may be influenced by national and international perspectives.

Overview

The nature of worldwide economic, ethical, social, political and technological challenges means that teachers' professional capabilities have to be more extensive and more honed than at any time hitherto. Teachers now have to meet expectations that their colleagues in earlier times never had to face. Most of this is also true of staff who support teachers.

They are required to sustain a continuous cycle of enhanced academic standards, prepare students for the multi-task/multi-opportunity worlds of work and leisure, help students to make sense of the accelerating information and communication revolution, play their part in developing students as 'rounded individuals' and competent, caring citizens, and give general support to those students who may spend most or all of their years of schooling in areas of deprivation and social distress. This chapter looks at the role of school leaders in increasing teachers' professional capabilities to meet these formidable national and global challenges.

Start with the 'vision'

'Be bold in what you stand for and careful what you fall for.'

Ruth Boorstin

In challenging times effective schools are effective because they are clear about:

◆ their context and what they wish to do for their students;
◆ what they are about as a community, including a shared educational vision and purpose;
◆ their day-to-day aims and objectives;
◆ the appropriate professional standards for them;
◆ the key policies that need to be in place to highlight and sustain those standards;
◆ the agreed 'whole school' strategies (academic, pastoral and professional) that help individual teachers to work towards the standards;
◆ the specific standard or quality of work that is expected from each member of staff;

◆ how students are helped to understand the relevance of the school's standards and the role they play in monitoring and reviewing these;

◆ what the staff know about the point the school is at in meeting the professional standards it has set.

It is this sense of overall purpose that enables school leaders to manage, not only the learning and development of the pupils, but also the professional development of staff. Schools that feel overwhelmed by external intiatives are unable to establish their own needs and therefore the needs of the staff within the school. There is no room for a 'victim' mentality in schools that are determined to develop. Thus, the starting point for an effective professional development programme is the establishment (or revisiting) of the aims of the school. Such a journey will ensure that themes and standards of professional development are united with the school's mission and key objectives. This fusion is more likely to be achieved when the leadership group:

◆ maps individual and organisational goals alongside ways of preserving some individual and team autonomy, so that the two aspects of practice are not regarded as incompatible;

◆ offers 360-degree feedback on professional performance for individuals, teams and the school as a whole;

◆ formalises the above two steps into an audit showing where individual members of staff and key teams are in their professional capability to meet the shared vision and goals;

◆ ensures that within the leadership team there is clear responsibility for staff development, including making tight links between 'whole school' strategies and professional development activities;

◆ places a strong emphasis on collaborative learning through shared planning, mentoring, task groups, action research and the exchange of best practice;

◆ encourages tasks groups to research ideas and identify good practice;

◆ integrates professional development activities within a general school culture in which self-evaluation and continuous improvement have high priority.

Acknowledge the pace of change

John Spencer

'Change is not an aberration, disturbing a normally stable world. Quite the reverse. There is **no** stability; change is **always** happening.'

The pace of change in education, and in the world generally, has meant that just to stand still requires energy and flexibility. **In little more than a decade** schools have had to take on the National Curriculum, local management, equal opportunities, revised health and safety arrangements, non-accidental injury issues, drugs education, sex education, the SEN code of practice, standard assessment tests, appraisal, formalised lesson observation, preparation for inspection by OFSTED, governing body training, performance management, benchmarking, baseline assessment, the national literacy strategy, the national numeracy strategy, Curriculum 2000 and above all the dramatic developments in ICT. It has become a cliché to observe that the only constant is change. All of these initiatives have been accompanied by centrally funded training, supplemented by further training funded from school budgets – and even from teachers' own pockets on occasions.

There is no point in school leaders not acknowledging the rate and pace of change and explaining why resistance occurs. The positive approach may be to distinguish clearly between what is statutory and what is not, but even what is statutory needs to be questioned (see the case studies in Chapter 3). It is also inevitable that all changes, however introduced and presented, have to be adapted to local circumstances and local resources. How best to achieve this contextualisation provides a natural agenda for each school to discuss the 'management of change'.

Though national education changes are presented as 'top–down' initiatives 'driven' through the governing body and headteacher, all experienced heads and governors know that the changes will be successfully implemented only when they are 'steered' through the staff and throughout the school. They also know that many staff have to be brought on board in the role of 'change agents' if momentum is to be sustained and progress achieved.

Issues in focus 8.1

The concept of the 'change agent' and what part they play in an organisation's cohesion and success has been much discussed in educational and general management literature in the past twenty years. It is generally accepted that any change agent is not a 'hero-innovator' working in isolation, but a member of staff who, because they have more understanding of the change process and change mechanisms, can act, when required, as a conduit or key point of contact in a change programme. They may undertake these functions for ↓

individuals or teams. The change agent will demonstrate and reinforce the organisation's commitment to a proposed change, but they cannot substitute for the lack of an overall plan.

The general characteristics of successful change agents have been clearly described. They cluster around four broad dimensions of the change process. These are:

◆ **positive disposition** – strong allegiance to 'their organisation'; in general agreement with the organisation's purpose and goals; a preparedness – even if realistically cautious – to let the 'old order' be replaced by an alternate; a willingness to learn; behaviours that overtly demonstrate a commitment to change; natural curiosity and measured risk-taking; in tune with people rather than in love with abstracts;

◆ **capacity for collegiality** – strong interpersonal skills; good judge of people's aspirations and difficulties; team player; full understanding of the interconnection between key roles, but also their separateness; skill at networking; respect from others for constructively challenging the existing culture when needed;

◆ **self-conviction** – knows own core values; capable of interacting with the 'power units' in the organisation for the benefit of all; tenacity to live with and manage risk; able to sustain energy for professional commitments and life in general;

◆ **knowledge of the system** – knows the key 'synaptic junctions' in the organisation's 'nervous system'; forecasts likely anxieties and pressure from change for individual people and for teams; sees clearly how the aims of the change programme relate to the structure of the organisation and its development goals.

No single individual will demonstrate all these characteristics for all of the time. Some of them can be nurtured in most staff, so that the school develops a reservoir of change agents as it develops its change project and its supporting programme of professional development.

Establishing the purpose of professional development

'This organisation needs to organise to reach closer agreement on what this organisation needs.'

Internet graffiti

The primary purpose of professional development is to move the school forward. The principal developments will be meeting more effectively the full range of educational needs and preparing the students for successful lives. Over the longer term the professional development offered to staff should be evaluated against these two key objectives, even though in the shorter term different elements of the core objectives will be represented in the school development plan. Equally, since successful professionals need to sustain drive and commitment, especially in times when the rate and pace of change is rapid, the professional development programme needs to be regularly reviewed against personal development goals and personal career targets.

Individual and institutional needs should be discussed and prioritised. This may mean the use of staff meetings and workshops to generate open-ended discussion about issues that need tackling within school, possible solutions, and the scope within the 'whole school' focus for individual members of staff to meet personal and professional development targets. Such discussion should help to establish a 'whole school' strategy for professional development. Performance management is then used to align all professional development initiatives at the centre.

Issues in focus 8.2

Performance management (PM) 'sets a framework for teachers and their team leader to agree and review [professional development objectives] within the overall framework of schools' development plans. It focuses on more effective teaching and leadership to benefit pupils, teachers and schools.'

DfEE 2000a, p. 1

At the time of going to press, it is apparent that all schools are somewhere along a wide continuum in their understanding and implementation of PM. The continuum is represented by five developmental categories. These are:

◆ **Policy awareness** General awareness of the need for a PM policy. Early discussion about its shape and format. Significant professional development still needed to refine the policy and start towards its implementation.
◆ **Embryonic development** Commitment to implementing the policy. Appropriate discussions with staff and governors. Some effective 'whole school' strategies evident. General principles, process and timescale agreed and known by staff. ↓

◆ **Developing policy** Formal adoption of a policy or near to closing on such. Definite links with professional development priorities and planning. Integrated strategy starting to come together. Internal performance monitoring systems align with policy.

◆ **Policy implemented** Policy in place and forms the basis of a coherent strategy for staff development. PM policy does not sit in isolation but forms part of a range of school development objectives.

◆ **Policy embedded** PM policy and its implementation fully integrated into the school's general and data management structures.

The DfEE sees PM as a process not an event. It involves:

◆ **Planning** Team leaders discuss and record priorities and objectives with each of the teachers in their team. They discuss how progress will be monitored.

◆ Monitoring The teacher and team leader keep progress under review throughout the cycle, taking any supportive action needed.

Figure 3: Performance management cycle

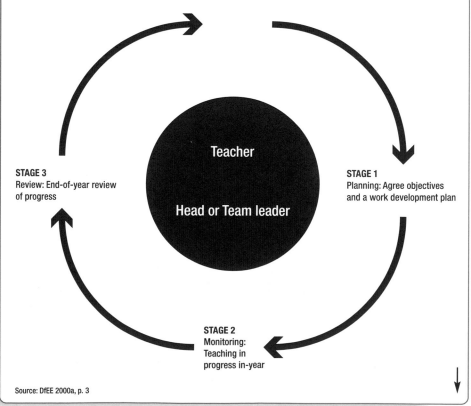

Source: DfEE 2000a, p. 3

◆ **Review** The teacher and team leader review achievements over the year and evaluate the teacher's overall performance taking account of progress against objectives.

The precise timing of the cycle is a matter for discussion and agreement within each school. The head will need to consider the workload implications and how the cycle will best fit with the school's other planning arrangements. After the first year, planning should flow naturally from the previous year's review.

DfEE 2000a, p. 5

The difference between this cycle and what has already been happening will vary considerably from school to school and LEA to LEA. For example, many schools were operating what might be called 'professional development reviews' involving an annual (or biannual) meeting with a line manager, with the interviewee's action plan as the focal point. Other schools went further and introduced lesson observation as part of an annual process – pre-empting the statutory 'minimum of one observation each year'.

Several readers will recognise many similarities with 'appraisal'. Regulations relating to the appraisal of teachers were in force throughout the 1990s and were reintroduced as statutory in 1999. However, in spite of the implied legal coercion, implementation was extremely patchy, with some schools producing full-blown schemes and others virtually ignoring the process. The resistance to appraisal revolved around three vital issues:

◆ historical resistance to classroom inspection;
◆ a possible link with pay;
◆ insufficient paid time for appraisal interviews to take place and insufficient time for lesson observations and accompanying feedback.

Performance management was also introduced without paid meeting/ observation time and with a clear link with pay. Some might argue that an ever-more tightly controlled government agenda has rendered teachers increasingly compliant. Others might say that performance management as a tool for developing teachers and raising standards of pupil attainment was long overdue.

The link between performance reviews and pay is by far the greatest and most contentious change from what went before. As the DfEE (2000a) puts it:

> 'The outcomes of performance review will be used to inform pay
> decisions, for example, for awarding double performance increments
> for outstanding performance up to the performance threshold, and
> for awarding discretionary pay performance points above the
> threshold, for Advanced Skills Teachers and teachers in the
> leadership group.'

p. 8

Just as significantly, the regulations introduce provision for using
performance review information in relation to 'dismissal or disciplinary
matters . . . where information from the review, **taken with other
material**, gives rise to concern about capability . . . it may lead to a
decision to investigate and record performance more intensively'. However,
'performance review interviews should not be used to administer warnings
in relation to dismissal or disciplinary procedures'.

DfEE 2000a, p. 9

DfEE 2000b, p. 4

In general, it is still too early to judge the effectiveness of the PM
initiative. If teachers are to see the performance process as a positive
system of help and support, and not a threat, the leadership group needs to
ensure that:

◆ PM draws on the true life and work of the school and is established
  within the school's general improvement planning.
◆ The school's PM cycle is well known by all.
◆ Teachers and the teams in which they work can identify progress
  through their usual planning and monitoring processes.
◆ Information about performance is drawn from a range of evidence –
  internal lesson observations, peer reviews, analysis of pupil
  achievement data, inspection findings, student and parent opinion,
  self-appraisal and team reflection and feedback.
◆ Appropriate reference is made to professional development criteria – for
  example that reflected in national, LEA and school-based professional
  standards.
◆ Targets set are stretching but realistic.
◆ Structured opportunities exist outside of PM for staff to discuss with
  line managers general development needs and career aspirations.
◆ The identified annual training and development needs do lead to
  appropriate professional development and training.

Developing potential

'Appreciate what you have before you haven't.'   Anonymous

In a world where good staff are nuggets of gold and losing them is
bereavement, helping them develop their potential can often seem a rather
masochistic process when they take off for promotion to another school.
However, a school that fails to develop talent will deprive itself of potential
for internal promotion and get a reputation for being unable to move
people on. This, in turn, means fresh blood is never injected and leads to
stagnation.

In structural terms, it is necessary to have in place suitable professional
development opportunities for all staff. This means a variety of different
types of activity. The most powerful learning that all teachers experience is
when they observe effective colleagues in action. A national culture that
says staff have to go off-site for their training should be questioned.
Several schools have developed – in partnership with other schools, the
LEA or the local higher education provider – change-specific and role-
specific packages that centre on in-house training. Some of these are
award-bearing – for example, a number of schools or school consortia
already offer in-house MA or MBA courses that are run in conjunction with
the local university. The potential of on-line learning is also being realised
as more and more study units for national professional qualifications are
offered by this means.

The range of professional needs to be covered in any school is already wide
and will become wider as expectations of teachers continue to increase and
as performance management indicates individual and collective
professional targets. The leadership group needs to be conscious of:

◆ the overall pattern of school and individual needs;
◆ the types of professional development best suited to the school staff and
the school development plan.

Identification of school needs

School needs, including some of the development needs of individual
members of staff, may be identified via various routes, for example, the
school development plan (and linked year and subject development plans),
OFSTED reports, professional development reviews/appraisals/performance

reviews, the use of survey methods and the use of self-review inventories relating to professional development. Senior managers need to be alert to the messages that come through to them from these sources about the long-term training needs of all staff. For example, if the achievement of boys has been identified as an area for attention, the necessary development programme is likely to run over a considerable period of time and require careful planning. The temptation, looking at the implications of such long-term planning, will be to go for quick fixes – but these rarely pay off.

There will be training needs that have to be met because of government initiatives, for example any curricular and pedagogical training required to meet literacy, numeracy and ICT targets. In these cases, school needs and external demands will come together.

In general, however, most schools will need to determine their own 'needs analysis' from the sources of information they have about the school's performance. Many schools do now have in place an annual training needs analysis (with top-ups at shorter intervals if required), with identified needs being clustered in line with the major dimensions of the school development plan and national targets.

Target audiences

Some schools have extended the needs analysis to cover **all employees**. Priorities are scaled across the range of staff, but three groups tend to get focused consideration.

Newly qualified teachers

However good their initial training programme may have been, it will not have prepared the newly qualified teacher for the pressures of an almost continuous full timetable (and its accompanying preparation, marking and pupil-contact load), break duties, after-school activities, meetings, links with parents and all the other activities that make up the hurly-burly of school life. The scope for the continuation of professional knowledge, understanding and skills into the early years of work has now been formalised through the **career entry profile** (TTA 2000). This, and the national statutory induction requirements, should form the basis of any school-focused support.

Teachers 'new' to the school

The needs of teachers 'new' to a school have tended to be neglected. As experienced teachers, they have been expected to swim (rather than sink) and 'just get on with it'. Such negligence can have disastrous consequences, with staff failing to become part of the wider school team because they have not understood the culture. Because they don't understand the culture they find the adjustment to the new job difficult and there is the potential for failing to engage with what the school stands for and how it operates. At worst, such poorly inducted staff quickly become hostile to their new environment.

Although there is no statutory scheme, as there is for NQTs, all schools should provide a written statement setting out the programme of induction and ongoing training that staff 'new' to the school (other than NQTs) are entitled to and can expect. Notice board 6 sets out one school's provision for new teaching staff who are not NQTs.

Notice board 6   Induction programme for new, but not newly qualified, teachers

Section 1

Procedures following appointment	Who is primarily responsible?		
	HT	**SMT link**	**HoD**
Notify LEA	*		
Letter of confirmation	*		
Set up pigeon hole/mailings		*	
Term dates		*	
Timetable		*	*
Arrange pre-service visits		*	*
School site		*	
Accommodation		*	
Arrangements for induction year		*	
'Whole school' policies, procedures, routines		*	*
Expectations of pupils		*	*

Notice board 6   Induction programme for new, but not newly qualified, teachers (cont.)

Procedures following appointment / Who is primarily responsible?

Procedures following appointment	HT	SMT link	HoD
Classroom and behaviour management		*	*
Teaching resources			*
Schemes of work			*
Lesson planning			*
Differentiation			*
Rewards and sanctions			*
Day-sheet and permission slips			*
Use of planners – communications with parents			*
Referral system			*
Record keeping, marking and assessment			*
Homework timetable			*
Type and quality of homework			*
Display			*
ICT			*
School and department improvement plan		*	*
Individual action plan			*
Classroom observation	*		
Pastoral duties			HoY
Assembly routines			HoY
School duties		*	
INSET application			HoD

Section 2   During first year

A programme of activities to be arranged prior to each year to occur during scheduled meetings after school and to include:

◆ classroom and behaviour management;
◆ time and stress management;

Notice board 6   Induction programme for new, but not newly qualified, teachers (cont.)

◆ school routines;
◆ marking;
◆ use of school resources;
◆ differentiation/mixed-ability teaching;
◆ evaluating your own teaching;
◆ role of form tutor;
◆ recognising achievement;
◆ parents' evenings;
◆ equal opportunities;
◆ improvement plans;
◆ continuing professional development;
◆ profiles;
◆ the role of HoY/HoD/SMT/headteacher (HT);
◆ meeting special educational needs.

During the first half of the autumn term new staff will have the opportunity to observe experienced colleagues in their own and other departments. Staff will be encouraged to observe colleagues throughout the first year and to visit other schools, focusing on predetermined areas. An individual programme will be negotiated with the SMT link responsible for staff development. In addition they will be attached to an existing member of staff or 'buddy' for informal help and support.

Heads of department will meet with the teacher at least once per fortnight during the first term, and thereafter monthly to review progress and set targets. These meetings will be set against supply/cover periods and the HoD will need to inform the administration staff responsible for cover of the period designated as meeting time.

Induction of newly qualified/probationary teachers will include lesson observations and feedback by both the HoD and the member of SMT linked to a department.

Wherever possible, newly qualified teachers will be released to attend central activities organised by The Teachers' Centre.

Induction programme supplied with kind permission of The Compton School

Support staff

Some schools pay lip-service to the importance of involving support staff in the school as a whole, others actually achieve it. However, in general, the reality is often far from the rhetoric, and support staff can find themselves isolated from the teaching staff and even from each other. Many support staff will never have worked in a school before and need proper induction into the characteristics not only of the school they are in but of schools in general. They also need training on the job just as much as teaching staff do. The world of constant change impacts on non-teaching staff such as administrators, clerical staff, technicians and caretakers as pressingly as it does on any other group of employees. Whether the topic be ICT, health and safety, the use of new materials or other topics, all support staff need to be up to date in order to fulfil their role.

Strategic PIN down – Reflection 8.1

Aims
- to ensure support staff are committed to the school's aims and ethos;
- to make adequate provision for the development needs of support staff.

P – State the PROBLEM	Support staff appear isolated from the teaching staff and from each other. To encourage their active support for school policy we need to . . .
I – Clarify the ISSUE	All staff, teaching and support, should feel they are one team with common aims. To get to this state we are . . .
N – Tackle the NEED	To verify how far support staff understand the school's aims and agree with them we propose to . . .

Before you begin, think about:

- how best to get an accurate indication of the views of support staff;
- the extent to which criticism may be invited by canvassing views;
- what action is possible to deal with criticism;
- what the budgetary implications might be of any changes.

Tip
Don't raise expectations that cannot be fulfilled.

Promoting effective professional learning and development

'Put as much thought to sowing ideas as to reaping achievements.'
Company slogan

For most teachers their first taste of professional development after completing their initial training comes when they apply for a job. Comparing the responses to a number of applications can be highly illuminating. Some 'appointment packs' will generate instant excitement, others will appear to have been put together in a hurried and half-hearted manner. And these differences are found at every level, up to and including headship. For example: the new school headship in outer London that was in the *Times Educational Supplement* as a cheap twelve-line lineage advertisement – surrounded by expensive 'boxed' items; the 'pack' for the headship of another new school in the West Country gave no information about the appointment process or the budget, and the application form had been so hurriedly stuffed into an envelope that it arrived looking creased and battered.

Of course, differences between packs of written information will not necessarily reflect differences between schools 'on the ground', but they will provide clues that need to be followed up. Ideally, the excitement experienced on the first reading of a job description will be built upon as each stage of the process unfolds until, eventually, you realise that this really is a genuine reflection of the school itself and how it operates. Good practice should include the following:

◆ concise, well-written descriptions of the job and the school;
◆ a clear description of how the appointment process will take place;
◆ the involvement of relevant staff, for example the role of key line managers;
◆ a rigorous, but fair, appointment process, for example no assessment based on how you tackle the lunchtime buffet with staff and governors;
◆ sensitivity towards unsuccessful candidates and the offer of feedback;
◆ positive arrangements between appointment and starting, for example, more information about the school, pupils and future colleagues;
◆ letter of appointment/salary details all worked through and communicated promptly;
◆ some details about the school's professional development programme.

If you are reading this from the perspective of managing a school or school team, and you can 'tick' all the above, then you have managed the first stage of induction and professional development for your new staff. They will know what the school's values are, how it operates and, most importantly, what potential there is for them to contribute and make a difference.

The learning that takes place before staff even take up their posts will have built up expectations of what may come in terms of further learning and development 'on the job', including formal training utilising the school's INSET budget. And with budgets in many schools cut to a minimum (those early 'grant-maintained' days when heads found their INSET pots so large that they could never spend all the money in them seem far away), it is crucial to ensure that expenditure on training provides value for money. To this end it is worth staff identifying **how best they learn**.

Encouraging professional reflection

This is the cheapest way of developing professionally. Unfortunately, it is also, without structure and funding, one of the hardest. Constructive reflection is not easy to achieve and there are always 'things to do' that seem more pressing than mere contemplation.

However, reflection on past successes and failures and identifying what works and what doesn't work will be built into any good training programme. A leading teacher-trainer told the story at a staff training session of how, in his second year as a teacher-trainer, he came up with a number of ways the course might be improved. When he put these to an elderly senior lecturer the reply was along the lines of: 'What do you know? You've only been here five minutes.'

Knowing that the senior lecturer in question should have been put out to grass years ago, our teacher-trainer ventured the following: 'You may have been working here for 20 years but all you've really done is to repeat your first year twenty times over.' Arrogant maybe, but a story that suggests that by itself experience is no guarantee of successful reflection on how to improve practice.

Issues in focus 8.3

Reflective knowledge is built from a variety of sources of evidence. In a professional context, it emerges by considering what has been done, the interactions that have taken place, the responsiveness of those involved, the impact of the activities or actions and so on. It also means connecting this range of information with one's own inner values about the quality of what has been done and why. It is, therefore, not instant knowledge. It derives from accumulation of evidence about professional performance. This is then applied to make amendments to oneself, one's professional approach and the performance of the team(s) and institution to which one belongs. It will, of course, be ever-changing knowledge as the dynamics of professional life unfold.

In cognitive terms, the processes involved are similar to those connected with the general interpretation of meaning – description, comprehension, summary, analysis, categorisation, explanation, elucidation and reconsideration.

West-Burnham and O'Sullivan (1998) describe reflective practice and offer a personal inventory of diagnostic questions. Field *et al*. (2000) consider how reflective knowledge relates to subject leadership. Schon (1983) outlines the general characteristics of the 'reflective practitioner'.

Evaluation – formal and informal

'Evaluation' has become a modern industry in its own right. It is not uncommon to see someone observing someone observing someone else. 'QAing' (quality assuring) is a term that has found its way into the lexicon of teacher jargon. All government-inspired initiatives seem to be accompanied by elaborate feedback structures. The theory is fine. Standards are being checked. Those under the microscope are being made responsible for their actions. However, the reality can often be far from this. OFSTED inspections, for example, are intended to provide schools and their staffs with feedback on their performance in order to help them improve. And of course, this is exactly what does happen in many instances. Sadly, in many others, inspections are carried out by people who do not have sufficiently intimate and detailed knowledge of the work of those they are inspecting to be able to make reliable judgements. Stories of excellent staff being intimidated, indeed frozen, by OFSTED are legion.

And there are as many more whose performance should have been found wanting but wasn't.

This said, constructive feedback on performance can be invaluable and really help staff move forward. Evaluations do not have to be formal, structured or regular and there is a place for 'one-offs', which, timed appropriately, can be just as powerful. How many of us remember the 'word in the ear' that changed our view of ourselves and thus our behaviour? Sometimes such informal evaluations may come from pupils: 'Sir/Miss. Why do you always . . . ?' or 'Sir/Miss. Why do you never . . . ?' If only one could work with an invisible, trusted, friendly trainer on the shoulder who would know just the moment to pass comment!

Self-evaluation is gradually taking over from the formal helicoptering in of inspectors, although, outside teaching, such an approach is not new. Perhaps the term 'helicoptering in' came from the way British health and safety teams used to operate on oil rigs in the North Sea. Their approach (as with OFSTED) was to give notice of a visit. This is in turn triggered frenzied preparations in order to make sure everything was in order for the arrival of the inspectors' helicopter. Once all had been passed, things could go back to normal! The Norwegians, on the other hand, saw their role as being to check the rig's **self-evaluation** procedures, that is, what structures were in place for ensuring the health and safety of employees and what means were used **by the workers** to monitor these procedures.

In the past there has been some suspicion of self-evaluation. It was said that everyone always emerged smiling from it. However, this was before the introduction by the Secondary Heads Association (SHA) (Bennett 1999), the DfEE (1998) and others of the structured approaches we now see. Such structures allow, and encourage, genuine 'self-confrontation' to take place.

Lesson observations

Alongside an ever-increasing emphasis on evaluating teaching and learning, the introduction of performance management by the DfEE (2000a) has resulted in 'lesson observation' becoming the key issue for professional development in thousands of schools. Under PM all schools are being required to introduce annual lesson observations.

Nevertheless, there are thousands of teachers in the system whose teaching has never been observed by colleagues. Of course, very many of these have, through other means (e.g. examination results, reflections on practice, pupil and parent feedback) honed their skills to a fine point. Sadly, there are some, sometimes those nearing the end of their careers, who have developed little since they started because they have never fully understood their strengths or confronted their weaknesses.

As usual, government regulations tell you what to do but not how to do it. A structured programme of lesson observation is likely to mean time away from classes for the observer and time required for feedback for both observer and the colleague observed. As we have already noted, appraisal never took off – because of unrealistic demands on time as much as because of objections to the principle. Whether more formal lesson observations will develop best practice remains to be seen.

It has to be said that many schools have shied away from internal lesson observations because of the tensions the introduction of such a scheme can engender. Partly this is the OFSTED connection, partly the actual assigning of observers to observees (with known, not necessarily friendly, people appearing in your classroom) and partly a lack of clarity as to what is being observed and how comments will be fed back and subsequently used. As with 'threshold assessment', there is considerable potential for PM to undermine the harmonious and collegiate approach that so many schools have worked on successfully for so long. To prevent this happening, the leadership group needs to ensure that:

◆ lesson observations are reported objectively, but within an ethos of 'improving on previous best';
◆ all observations on the life and work of the school contribute to a self-critical professional review by the school as a whole;
◆ the school identifies and celebrates strengths – and goes beyond merely putting things right;
◆ the merits of controversial or competing practices are fully discussed;
◆ the practice in the school benefits from that seen elsewhere.

In-class support

In many schools there will be 'in-class support' – usually funded through special needs funding, although there may well be standard funds that are targeted at particular groups of pupils. Of course, the principal role of the support teacher is to work with designated pupils, and any suggestion that the role might be broadened to include commenting on the performance of the class teacher would be quite inappropriate. However, if the support teacher and the class teacher are working together as they should, they are likely to develop a sufficiently open and trusting relationship to enable them to analyse lessons together and identify where approaches work and where they do not. If no such exchanges take place, real opportunities for development are lost. Thomas *et al.* (1998) consider in depth the use of 'support' in inclusive classrooms.

Meetings

Chapter 7 looked at meetings in some detail (see pp. 157–8). In the context of the professional development of staff, they are central – providing as they do the most frequent way in which staff can reflect on their practice and learn from each other. Effective heads of faculty/department/house will organise their meetings, be they weekly or monthly, with great care in order to ensure that every aspect of their work is moved forward as much as possible – for the benefit of all students. Team leaders who appear to be neglecting the central role that regular meetings have in the life of the school need to be called to account. How many headteachers have experienced a familiar sinking feeling when one of their heads of year emerges from a meeting of his team 45 minutes before most other groups in the school and says something along the lines of: 'Well, Head, we've managed to get through all the business really efficiently. No one had any issues they wanted to bring up and there's no point in sitting around for the sake of it, is there?' In such circumstances, as headteacher, you should have ready your own mental list of issues/items that you can suggest it would have been very useful for that team to discuss.

Notice board 7   What effective team leaders will discuss to enhance staff and student performance

How can we create and sustain a team culture? What do we intend our students to know, understand and be able to do? What student feedback are we getting? Do we need more or a different type of feedback? How do our students see us? How do our colleagues see us? What do we have to cover as statutory? Where do we have most scope for creativity? What specialised techniques are we using/could we be using? Do we have sufficient planned variety in lessons/units of work? How would we describe our best practice? Are we in line

---

Notice board 7   What effective team leaders will discuss to enhance staff and student performance (cont.)

with the school development plan? Is **our** development planning effective? Do we know how well we are doing? Are we making best use of examination results and other information about attainment? Are the links between staff and SMT open and positive? When 'push comes to shove' how are we monitoring the effectiveness of the team? How do we facilitate professional development? How could we do all of the above better?

Strategic PIN down – Reflection 8.2

Aims

◆ to reflect on the ways in which you have developed as a leader and manager;

◆ to identify strengths that you can develop in others;

◆ to identify areas for your own development.

P – State the PROBLEM	Heads find it difficult to get reliable feedback on their own performance unless . . .
I – Clarify the ISSUE	Training and developing effective leaders and managers is challenging. To ensure both time and school funds are used effectively . . .
N – Tackle the NEED	Who can we involve in providing accurate feedback and positive training?

Before you begin, think about:

◆ who and what you have learnt the most from;

◆ how your experience and the experiences of your colleagues can be used for the benefit of staff as a whole.

Tip

Talk to other heads and team leaders about their training experiences and training programmes.

Discussions: staff, like pupils, learn by talking

We can all probably remember animated staffroom discussions on educational issues. Is it a trick of our memories or are such discussions much less frequent? Certainly, the pace of work, in education as elsewhere, has speeded up dramatically. Conversations have always tended towards the functional and the brief, but, as we start the new millennium, they seem ever more so. Anything beyond 'Could you drop that list into me while I'm registering 9X', or 'I'll let you have the names of the pupils we're not entering at all', will probably be termed a meeting. Anything beyond day-to-day practicalities needs to be scheduled as an agenda item at a specific meeting.

But 'discussion' is important. It is a significant means by which we learn, and there are a number of ways in which discussion (or opportunities for discussion) can be facilitated – and blocked. There are some heads, for example, for whom the notion of staff discussion is quite threatening – linked, in their minds, with opportunities for 'management bashing'. A minority of such heads have, as a crude tactic to discourage discussion, dispensed with staffrooms altogether. Such behaviour is more likely to act as a self-fulfilling prophesy than a deterrent. On the other hand, providing opportunities for open discussion is likely to increase the sense of a school community. The discussions themselves will range from the personal to the professional, from football to Fullan, and will contribute to a positive atmosphere, appreciated by staff and frequently commented upon by outsiders.

Facilitating discussion might include the provision of reasonable breaks both mid-morning and lunchtime (not forgetting the stress that overlong lunchtimes create in so many schools) as well as pre-school, morning 'briefings' in the staffroom. These provide, as a positive spin-off, excellent opportunities for staff to deal with day-to-day issues. In a school of any size such opportunities are hard to come by.

For many staff it is impossible to get to the staffroom twice a day, and their formal interactions will be with those teaching closest to them – hopefully members of their own department. A dynamic and effective department will be talking to each other all the time, and the learning opportunities for staff (particularly for newly qualified teachers) are immense. To facilitate these invaluable interactions, departments need to have offices that are large enough for all members to be based in, to meet in and to house easily accessible resources. In this way, departmental members are likely to engage in *ad hoc* interaction with colleagues a number of times a day – an invaluable contribution to professional development.

Whilst purpose-built departmental bases are vital to the health of a department in that they encourage discussion and provide a location for accessible resources, isolationism does have to be guarded against, and this is where we come back to the staffroom. If it is welcoming and accessible, staff will try to use it – especially at morning break when tea or coffee are dispensed in a civilised manner, and even more so if you introduce rituals, such as cakes on Friday. The alternative, a rather crude one, is to collect up all departmental kettles and throw them on a skip!

Line management

Effective line management provides invaluable opportunities for training and development. Clearly, the 'managed' will benefit through a process of structured support and accountability – ideally from a senior colleague who has enjoyed successful experience her/himself. Equally, the line manager will need to ensure that precious time is well used, and this requires a high degree of preparation for each meeting as well as efficient follow-up. It also requires reflection on what it is that makes for effective department/team leadership and how that leadership can be developed for the good of all pupils.

To establish an effective line-management structure requires a serious investment in time. One possible model will see meetings taking place each half-term, according to a common agenda agreed by senior managers and allowing time for items to be raised by those they manage. Once a cycle of meetings has taken place, minutes will be discussed and issues requiring an SMT input will be dealt with. Although such an approach may sound relatively small scale, the logistics are actually quite formidable. First, SMT time needs to be given to producing a common agenda. Second, the line-management (link) meetings need to be scheduled to take place within a specified period (say two weeks). This is particularly challenging if, for example, you line-manage six departments/year teams and therefore need to find six significant slots (ideally timetabled periods of between 45 minutes and an hour). Third, further SMT time needs to be set aside for follow-up, otherwise momentum is lost.

The benefits of such a scheme are considerable. The managers and the managed work on developing good practice – the best of which provides a role model for staff across the board.

Strategic PIN down – Reflection 8.3	**Aim**
	◆ to provide all staff with a line manager who both supports and holds accountable those she/he line-manages.

P – State the PROBLEM	Staff are not clear how to carry out their roles or to whom they are accountable. First action is . . .
I – Clarify the ISSUE	An effective line-management structure provides support and accountability and ensures consistent implementation of school policy. We have achieved this by . . .
N – Tackle the NEED	Training line managers to focus on policy and performance in order that they can both support staff and make them accountable requires . . .

Before you begin, think about:

◆ how often line-management meetings should take place;
◆ what the agendas should be for these meetings;
◆ how you can be sure that what people say is happening is really happening;
◆ the balance between individuals and consistency across the school.

Tip
Arrange for a middle and senior management discussion about the purpose and value of a more structured line-management system before making any changes.

Reviewing

> 'Reviewing is a process through which individuals can reflect on past performance, consider their present situation and feelings and identify future action, potential and needs.'

TTA 1998

Reviewing is a variation on the line-management structure described above. It describes one way in which line management can take place. Whereas normally the line-management structure concentrates on specific areas of responsibility – say, on the role of the middle manager as a head of department/head of year – and excludes (because of time) the other contributions that those staff may be making to the school – the review/preview approach takes every aspect of the senior manager's role and assesses it in the light of performance against the reviewee's agreed targets. Such meetings might take place at the beginning and/or end of term, when what has been achieved over the previous term will be discussed and targets/action will be planned for the following term.

'Reviewing' as a process is contrasted with both 'coaching' and 'mentoring'. West-Burnham and O'Sullivan (1998) and Pearce (1998), amongst others, have described the important role that reflection plays in the reviewing process.

Coaching

Coaching as a leadership style (see Chapter 2) supports the long-term development of staff. It is set against **pace-setting**, which describes a kind of 'I'll show you how it's done' approach. The pace-setter is likely to disappear over the hill leaving colleagues gasping in her/his wake.

For our purposes, coaching can be thought of more simply in terms of helping colleagues improve their performance in relation to a particular issue or responsibility. The approach taken should be very much one of 'enablement', by providing feedback on what the individual has done in a way that opens up discussion and may lead to them identifying better ways of tackling the problem for themselves. Coaching can be used in lots of different situations, ranging from feedback on lesson observation (see the Forest Oak case study in Chapter 3) to unplanned situations where particular problems have arisen (the head's coaching of the NQT in managing a difficult pupil in the Bridge Market case study). One use is in relation to ICT – showing someone how to use Powerpoint for example. Another common use is in 'handovers', where, for whatever reason, one member of staff is taking on a responsibility that another member of staff is relinquishing. Examples of such handovers might be the organisation of a major school trip or the annual open evening. Such handovers are not only development opportunities for staff; properly handled they also ensure that a structure that has been painstakingly built up, maybe over a period of years, is not put back to zero to be planned again from scratch.

Needless to say any coaching has to be properly planned and sensitively handled. If it is not, there are likely to be recriminations from staff who feel ignored because they haven't been asked to be coaches, or staff who feel patronised because they feel they're being talked down to.

There is a considerable amount of literature on coaching. In particular, Mumford (1993) has written extensively on the use of coaching, and mentoring, in industry and commerce.

Mentoring

As with coaching and reviewing, mentoring also involves a particular relationship with another member of staff. The difference in this case is that the relationship does not require the 'expert' input that a coach would provide. It is also likely to be less formal than reviewing. The focus is on a more skilled or experienced person acting as role model, adviser, counsellor and friend. Typically, newly qualified teachers in schools will have a 'mentor' – often referred to as a 'buddy' to indicate the difference between this relationship and that with, say, a line manager.

'Buddy' systems in schools sometimes break down because the very term suggests a level of informality that invites an 'as and when' approach. However, a structured approach to mentoring can provide staff with an important source of support and development that is not easily available elsewhere in the school.

All three activities provide opportunities for staff to receive feedback and support and to reflect on their work in a way that enables them to move forward. As such, however they are organised, they are essential ingredients in any school's staff development programme.

For reviewing, coaching and mentoring to be effective strategies, those adopting them must possess a high degree of emotional intelligence (see Chapter 4). By the same token, it is likely that emotional intelligence will be developed in the reviewer and the reviewed, the coach and the coached, and the mentor and the mentored.

Shadowing and learning from positive role models

This is one of those fantasies we tend to indulge: 'If . . . [name of government education minister or LEA director of education or any other important but 'out of touch' person] did my job for a week, they'd soon realise just how ridiculous the demands being made on us are!' There is an element of revenge in shadowing fantasies – 'I know they'd suffer if they had to do my job.' However, shadowing can be an excellent way of gaining an insight into the world of work outside of education. 'Partners in leadership' is a scheme managed by the DFES for Business in the Community (a national 'not for profit' organisation) that links headteachers with their counterparts in business, and for many the experience is a rewarding one. Particular areas of common interest are finance, personnel, site management and, of course, staff development. One very positive spin-off of such an arrangement is the opportunity for the business person to witness at first hand the immensely demanding and complex nature of the head's work. Alternatively, shadowing can take place within schools or across schools. Although the experience is likely to be more predictable, you are more likely to be able to exploit the experience if you have been shadowing in a familiar situation.

A very effective approach to the development of middle management, and one which operates in many schools, is to arrange for middle managers to become members of senior management on a temporary, rota, basis. If senior management team meetings take place after school, there are no cover costs and the benefits are considerable on both sides: the middle managers get a real insight into the running of the school and the SMT expands both its thinking power and its links back to the rest of the staff. The same approach can be applied to those below the middle management level, by arranging for them to attend middle management meetings, although because these meetings are less frequent the arrangement has less impact. If this approach is used, it is essential that the senior management meeting, or activity being shadowed, models effective practice.

Visits to other schools

If the aim is to look at good educational practice elsewhere, a visit to another school – carefully planned and with sufficient staff involved to be able to share the experience – can be valuable. Teaching is still a very insular profession, taking place mainly within the four walls of the classroom, and opportunities for sharing good practice are not easy to come by. The DFES's 'Beacon School' programme should be helping to break down some of the barriers, although like so many central initiatives it was launched with insufficient attention to the 'how' – the potential conflict between, on the one hand, proclaiming your excellence and, on the other, sharing your expertise. Seekers after good practice should look for Beacon Schools that show some humility!

LEA advisers and inspectors have traditionally tried to use INSET days to bring staff from different schools together. Such days, if well-planned, can bear fruit. However, the fact that large groups of teachers bring such a variety of angles and experiences militates against a 'one size fits all' approach.

Twilight sessions in school

Most schools will, at some stage, set up 'twilight' INSET for their staff. Many of these sessions will deal with the introduction of statutory measures, such as threshold assessment and the literacy hour, and can cause resentment amongst staff already tired at the end of another long and demanding day. However, twilight sessions are an opportunity for responding to staff's expressed development needs, for example, timetabling, finance, job applications. They will not mind giving up an hour-and-a-half after school if the programme is in **response to their own requests**.

External INSET programmes

With such a plethora of initiatives raining down on teachers, many ex-teachers have decided that there are richer pickings and an easier life in providing courses and conferences for their erstwhile colleagues. The quality of people running such courses is very variable, ranging from the 'cowboy' to the highly sought-after speaker with an international reputation. Prices can vary – and do not include any cover that may have to be provided back at school. Ideally, albeit expensively, you send at least two people on any course so that they have someone to talk through the experience with and help them structure the reporting back to relevant staff. However, with a properly planned 'cascade', one person can pass on benefits to many other staff.

'What courses has she/he been on?' Job applicants always used to, and to an extent still do, agonise over what they can put in the box on the application form that shows their level of activity and their priorities in terms of formal training programmes. In truth, the interviewing panel can sometimes learn quite a lot from seeing what appears in these boxes. Nevertheless, the process of appointing staff has become more sophisticated, and any negatives in the INSET section can quite easily be cancelled out elsewhere. The motive for 'going on a course' should not, then, simply be to improve one's CV but also to benefit the school, that is, both individual and 'whole school development'.

Strategic PIN down – Reflection 8.4	**Aim**	
	◆ to advise staff on where they may get the best training.	
	P – State the PROBLEM	The quality of INSET provided outside the school is variable and frequently does not justify the funds allocated. We need to . . .
	I – Clarify the ISSUE	Staff get few opportunities to attend external courses and such courses are frequently costly. Resources (including staff time) should be used as effectively as possible, and INSET should be as practical as possible. We ensure this by . . .
	N – Tackle the NEED	We build up and use a file on the quality of external INSET providers in the following way . . .

Before you begin, think about:

◆ surveying staff experiences of INSET, both in your school and in colleagues' schools;
◆ finding out what training and development experiences staff have benefited from most;
◆ the extent to which training can be 'in-house'.

Tip
Think about whose views you trust and value.

External advisers and consultants

The process of slimming down LEAs over the past ten years or so has left inspector/adviser provision focused on the primary sector in most areas, and there is no doubt that the quality of such support, although inevitably erratic, is appreciated by thousands of primary headteachers. The same is not true in the secondary sector, where a dearth of LEA personnel with senior management experience has left secondary schools in many authorities feeling unsupported. There are, of course, still subject specialists in all LEAs, with schools 'buying in' to valued individuals rather than to a whole package.

Writing as consultants (albeit with good school management experience) we would not want to deny a role for ourselves in the current educational scene! However, our advice to schools would be to counsel caution when considering bringing in an expensive outsider. Before taking such a step you need to be sure that there is the best possible match between what the consultant can offer and your needs. This can only be done by 'taking up references' on your consultant, that is, making sure you can get some first-hand reports on her/his qualities.

Some external consultancy, such as that linked to performance management or headteachers' targets, will be 'free' (at least initially). But this shouldn't stop schools:

◆ finding out if they have a choice of consultant;
◆ exercising the choice if they have one.

Working parties

Working parties are an excellent way of providing development opportunities for staff. First, the actual issue being dealt with may well have been suggested by staff (as opposed to the head or the SMT) and there will, therefore, be considerable commitment to it. Second, providing the issues reflect the priorities of a sufficiently large number of staff, there will be enthusiasm to take part and contribute.

Schools will vary greatly in the extent to which their staffs wish to give up time to be on a working party. Careful thought needs to be given to balancing school needs (which staff would contribute most to this group?) and individual needs (which staff would learn/develop most from being on this group?). There is potential here for 'noses being put out of joint' and 'backs being put up'.

Action research

The concept of action research was explored in the first book in the series. Much said there is of relevance here. What is important is for schools and teachers to appreciate how much of their work mirrors 'research strategy' and the potential they have for systematic lines of enquiry in the course of their day-to-day work.

Leaders will wish to explore any use of the term 'research' that causes hackles to rise in overworked and 'stressed-out' staffrooms. It may do this if it implies intervention by some university-based academic who is not faced with the daily challenge of expectant (even resistant) faces waiting for the lesson to start. The essential approach is to show links with the kinds of activity that teachers in schools already engage in. The advantage of action research is that it provides a systematic way of getting at an issue. Too often in schools issues are taken up on the basis of a few loud, or powerful, voices, without sufficient attention being paid to any evidence that might be available in support of the views expressed.

Typically, a piece of action research will be set up on the basis of agreed identification of a problem – say, for example, 'Seating arrangements for pupils in lessons'. The teacher, or teachers, concerned will decide what information they want to collect, how they are going to collect it and, crucially, how they are going to process it. It is not uncommon for action research to founder at this point as the researchers find themselves overwhelmed with data. Assuming the stage has been achieved successfully, there are, hopefully, conclusions to be drawn and the potential for an 'action plan'. The plan is drawn up and implemented and the cycle starts all over again.

Action research may well provide opportunities for links with higher education institutions. DfEE (2000d) gives examples of some successful collaborative projects. Readers may well point to well-established programmes of monitoring, evaluation and review in their schools, and there will indeed be many similarities between some aspects of such programmes and action research.

Role models – positive and negative

We have already referred to role models (see 'Line management', pp. 185–6). All staff learn from role models. However, they learn far faster from how to do it than from how not to do it. The role of the head in ensuring that schools provide new, and existing, staff with positive role models is crucial. Nothing is more painful than to see an excellent newly qualified teacher fail to realise her/his potential because they find themselves in an underperforming, poorly led area of the school. In Chapter 6 we looked at dealing with 'marginal performers', and there is no doubt that marginal performers in middle or senior management positions cause damage not only by failing to carry out their responsibilities but also by the example they set for others.

What sort of learner are you?

When we establish schemes of work at school we consider the range of student learners we are catering for. It is helpful to apply the same considerations to adult learners – possibly starting with ourselves. For example, we are used to listening to lectures (and giving them) and yet research shows that, on average, only 5% of a lecture is retained by the listener, thus putting this form of teaching right at the bottom of the effectiveness table. At the other end of the scale is 'teaching others' and/or 'the immediate use of learning', with a 90% effectiveness rating (see Figure 4).

Figure 4: The Learning Pyramid: average retention rates

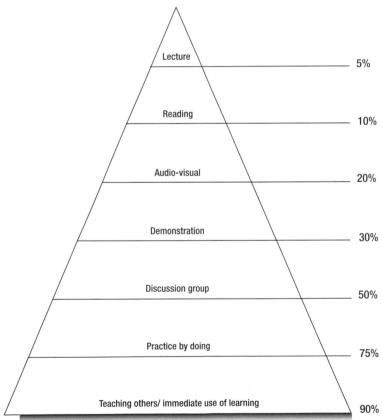

Source: Adapted from National Training Laboraties, Bethel, ME

It is important to know how you and your staff learn best in order to adapt your own internal INSET programmes and also to make appropriate demands on any visiting INSET provider. Such considerations will also help assess the likely usefulness of an external programme.

Staff development co-ordination

Every school needs to have a senior member of staff responsible for staff development. Ideally, this person is part of the SMT – in order that both on paper and in practice real importance is attached, and seen to be attached, to this role. In large schools, because staff development encompasses the very wide range of activities already referred to in this chapter, there is a temptation to create a 'one responsibility' post somewhere between senior and middle manangement. While such a post recognises the onerous nature of the work involved (including managing the funding of staff development), it may not give it sufficient status.

The staff development coordinator will, *inter alia*, have responsibility for tapping into staff expertise, putting opportunities in front of staff, and establishing and overseeing the staff development budget.

Tapping into staff expertise

'Home-grown' programmes, for example, the induction of new staff, are excellent opportunities for public recognition of the talent that you have within the school. To be asked to deliver part of a programme of training is highly motivating and generates the feeling throughout the staff as a whole that there is a powerful team and that there is recognition, at the highest level, of the individual strengths of that team. The appointment to membership of working parties (see p. 192) provides another excellent opportunity for public recognition of staff expertise.

As we have said, a cost in terms of time is attached to all activities, and any requests to staff to be involved in training need to go hand-in-hand with a time allowance. This will recognise, and attempt to compensate for, the pressures your staff are under.

Putting opportunities in front of staff

Staff need to know what training opportunities are available to them, and generally they will not have time to find this out. Mechanisms need to be in place to ensure that staff know what is available and what they have to do to avail themselves of development opportunities.

The co-ordinator's role, in relation to what comes into school from outside, is that of 'gatekeeper'. It is not in anyone's interests to be overwhelmed by junk mail. In fact, before anything reaches your co-ordinator it should have passed through the hands of a responsible person in the school office who will be able to bin the occasional obvious 'no-no' and will not be bothering any other member of senior staff with the mountain of mail generated by would-be providers of training.

The co-ordinator should have a sizeable board in the staffroom on which to pass on information about training courses. This will include, for example, information about LEA courses – in those areas where they are being run. Some authorities will publish voluminous handbooks each year, but what appears in these is not necessarily what actually takes place. Often, the publicising of such courses parallels the publicising of the advisory services. This is what we have on offer – provided you buy into it. Many advertised courses do not take place.

It is the role of the co-ordinator not only to make sure that information gets through to the right people, but also to build up her/his knowledge of what may, or may not, be worth spending money on. We have already referred to 'cowboy' operators. There needs to be a list of reliable providers and a blacklist of those to be avoided.

Finally, all staff need to be reminded that, when costing staff development, both the cost of the course and of the cover have to be taken into consideration.

Establishing and overseeing staff development budgets

Funding for staff development needs to be discussed each year as part of the budget planning process. The main issue will be to determine the extent to which the DFES's standards funding, being passed on from the LEA, should be supplemented. The answer to this will depend on a number of factors, for example:

◆ the extent of the standards funding (this in turn will depend on the socio-economic circumstances of the LEA);
◆ the health or otherwise of the school budget;
◆ the school's needs.

A process of analysis will result in an amount (additional to the standards fund) being identified in the school budget. At this point the staff development co-ordinator will need to decide how this 'pot' is to be divided up. In order to do this she/he might establish a working party, thus giving overt recognition to the importance of development opportunities for staff. And, of course, as we have already said, being a member of such a working party is in itself a significant opportunity for staff development.

Finally, both budgets – the staff development and the standards fund – need to be administered. In many schools this basic accounting job is still taken on by a senior member of staff, who is being paid far more than is necessary for this task and will probably not do it as well as your 'assistant bursar' in the school office.

Strategic PIN down – Reflection 8.5

Aim

◆ to establish a staff training and development budget that meets the needs of the widest possible range of staff within the context of the school aims and the school development plan.

P – State the PROBLEM	Staff are not clear how staff training is funded and feel insufficient resources are available to meet their personal needs.
I – Clarify the ISSUE	Successful schools will pay great attention to staff training and ensure that funding is adequate and is effectively targeted at school needs.
N – Tackle the NEED	Involve a cross-section of staff in decisions about funding of staff training and ensure that such decisions are transparent.

Before you begin, think about:

◆ how you will decide on the size of the overall 'pot';
◆ who is responsible for the training and development budget in the school;
◆ how a staff training committee/group/working party might be set up.

Tip
Aim for total transparency so that all funding decisions are covered by a policy and can be rationally explained.

How to disseminate the benefits of training

Staff development funding is a valuable resource, and a return has to be expected on the outlay – especially where staff go off-site to courses run by the LEA or private providers. If you can send two of your staff on a course, it will prove more cost-effective, as they will be able to sift through and shape feedback in a way that one person will find hard to do. However, since many staff attend a particular course or training programme as individuals, there needs to be a formal mechanism for ensuring feedback – whether in the form of a written report, which can be part of a regular bulletin, or a presentation to staff. The latter might be a session on an INSET day or simply a slot at a staff meeting. Another approach that can prove effective is to set up a 'mini' session for those staff interested in a particular issue.

Professional development for the headteacher

The phrase 'lead learner' has often been used in relation to heads. What does this mean? It confirms that the head is not exempt from the notion of 'lifelong learning'. There are many examples of people in all walks of life and at all ages learning new skills and acquiring knowledge, and these should act as a stimulus and spur to all of us. For many heads, the point at which they say 'No more change, no more initiatives, nothing more new' is the point at which they start to think of retiring from the fray. Equally, those heads who appear to have nothing more to learn will discourage others through their arrogance and lack of humility. So your training needs as head are just as great as those of any other member of your staff.

However, the notion of 'lead learner' goes beyond this. The managing director of a company might be seen as the lead learner, showing his employees he is prepared to confront the challenge of new knowledge and skills. What is different for schools is that their core function is learning, and if the head sees her/himself, and is seen, as a learner, this communicates itself to staff and pupils and helps to make the institution one where everyone is touched by the excitement of learning.

In fairness to heads, much of the training on offer has been less than helpful in that it has been provided either by trainers with little or no experience beyond that of middle management, or it has been provided by trainers who have been long since removed from the classroom and the school and whose understanding of the contemporary education scene is through paper rather than people.

However, there is now another dimension to training programmes for heads and aspiring heads. Hitherto, such programmes have concentrated on what leaders need to know and do. With the DFES's revised National Professional Qualification for Headship (NPQH) and the well-established Leadership Programme for Serving Heads (LPSH), there has been a shift towards developing the leadership skills and styles needed to create a shared vision that mobilises the commitment of all the stakeholders. LPSH provides each head with systematic feedback from some of those who work within the school. Through this, they can assess their impact on the climate of the school (see p. 33). For the vast majority of heads this has been a new experience. A few have found it very unsettling. Most have gained energy and direction as a result of holding up a mirror to themselves and seeing how they can develop their own leadership effectiveness.

Headteachers need to recognise and attend to their own needs. In that way they learn not just to deal with change but to shape it – and at the same time avoid 'burn-out'.

Improving the quality of education for all students

'There is no happiness for people at the expense of other people.'   Anwar el-Sadat

More than ever before there is national recognition of untapped student potential. We now have not only national league tables but international ones – many of which show Britain lagging behind other developed countries in a number of curriculum areas. There is a clear need to improve standards of education. Crucially, there is the belief, and the evidence, that it is possible to achieve improved standards.

Improved standards mean, above all, improving the quality of teaching in the classroom, and this must be the focus of programmes of professional development. However, a TTA (1995) survey of teachers indicated that only 26% of teachers thought that staff development impacted significantly on classroom practice. When we look at the 'what' and the 'how' of staff development, we need to keep this figure in mind. Staff development funds are scarce resources and accounting for their effective use must be rigorous.

Finally, the 'isolation' factor should be again mentioned. Teaching is still largely an insular occupation, with schools cut off from each other and the teachers within them operating mainly alone within the walls of their classrooms. Training programmes put staff, and schools, in touch with each other – to the point where course evaluations are often far more positive about the opportunities provided for interaction with colleagues than about the formal programme itself. Effective professional development recognises the contribution that informal teacher exchange makes to the learning progress. Describing, confirming, sharing and developing practice is actively encouraged.

Interesting facts 6   The teacher as reader

'Libraries are under threat, but the most rapidly disappearing of them all is the staffroom library. Ten years ago you could walk into almost any staffroom and there would be a few shelves of well-used books on such topics as children's backgrounds, school development and special needs – even the odd volume on moral issues or alternative schools.

Now, in all but a few, the same shelves are overloaded with official publications and outdated reference books.'

Eggleston 2000

What are the interesting facts about your staffroom library and you and your team as readers of professional literature? Are staffroom libraries no longer needed? Mail your response to yourself/selves, the headteacher, the governor, the trust, the LEA, or the secretary of state for education – whoever you think has the key to an adequate response.

Summary

Helen Keller

'Avoiding danger is no safer in the long run than outright exposure. The fearful are caught as often as the bold.'

◆ Effective schools continually re-examine their professional standards in the light of challenging and changing times.
◆ They are as sure as they can be about what changes they want to bring about. Equally, they are sure of the values they will not change.
◆ Many staff need to be nurtured as 'change agents' if the change process is to be welcome across the school.
◆ Any professional development programme in support of change has to take into account and balance both institutional and individual needs.

There has to be balance across strategic development, staff needs and staff interests.

◆ Performance management has the potential to be perceived by head and teachers as a professional support system. It needs to be developed as a management tool that enables all staff to see their own development in the light of 'whole school' targets, and the leadership group need to draw evidence from the best of collegial practice.

◆ Appropriate needs analysis, clarity about target audience and the matching of learning styles and methods to needs are essential prerequisites of effective professional development.

◆ A variety of opportunities and strategies are needed for all staff to engage in worthwhile professional learning and development.

These are challenging times for school leaders and their staff. Rapid technological and social change has made the task of educating young people more problematic. Classrooms and schools are in need of both high levels of craft expertise and fresh approaches to learning. The one factor that has remained constant has been government application of pressure on schools to raise standards and drive up achievement.

In our case studies of good practice and our examples of black spots, we have seen that the quality of leadership has been the critical internal influence in determining how well or how badly schools respond to these external pressures. There is no one way to be successful and many different ways in which poor or mediocre leadership can precipitate the downward spiral. But there are clear common themes that point the way forward. Long-term success is not achieved by the lone hero battling triumphantly against the odds. It happens when heads, by exercising intelligent spiritual, cognitive and emotional leadership, win over the hearts and minds of those they lead. Key characteristics of this leadership include:

◆ having and holding to a vision and set of values that transcend merely instrumental goals;
◆ keeping uppermost in everyone's mind the *raison d'être* of schools – the emotional, academic and social development of all students;
◆ treating all staff consistently and fairly;
◆ seeking to develop everyone's potential and providing opportunities for them to learn and improve both via feedback from coaching and from collaborative investigation;
◆ recognising and valuing staff efforts and achievements;
◆ showing a single-minded determination to stay on course, tackle issues of unacceptable standards of behaviour or performance and make sure that the things that should happen are happening;
◆ developing the capacity of all staff both to lead and to contribute to high-performing teams;
◆ aligning individual goals with organisational goals.

In demonstrating these behaviours school leaders will be using a range of leadership styles to create a positive climate where staff feel, like the teacher at Bridge Market, that the challenges they face in their work are ones they can meet, not problems that wear them down and diminish their self-belief. The primary task of schools is to develop each child's potential. The most effective way to bring that about is for school leaders to maximise the rich potential of their own staff.

Adair, J. (1987) *Effective Teambuilding*, London: Pan Books.

Adair, J. (1997) *Effective Leadership Masterclass*, London: Pan Books.

Armstrong, M. and Baron, A. (1998) *Performance Management: The New Realities*, London: Institute of Personnel and Development.

Barber, M. (2000) 'High expectations and standards for all – no matter what', edited version of speech delivered to Smith Richardson Foundation in Washington, reported in *Times Educational Supplement*, 7 July.

Barth, R. (1990) *Improving Schools from Within: Teachers, Parents and Principals Can Make the Difference*, San Francisco, CA: Jossey-Bass.

Bell, G. (1990) *The Secrets of Successful Business Meetings*, London: Heinemann.

Bennett, D. (1999) *Managing Self-Review*, Leicester: SHA Publications.

Bern, S. (1977) *Psychological Androgyny*, New York: West Publishing Company.

Blanchard, K. (1994) *The One Minute Manager Meets the Monkey*, London: HarperCollinsBusiness.

Blishen, E. (1969) *This Right Soft Lot*, London: Thames and Hudson.

Bottery, M. (1992) *The Ethics of Educational Management*, London: Cassell.

Boyatzis, R. (2000) 'What if learning were the purpose of education?', London Leadership Centre, Annual Lecture, Institute of Education, London University, 26 June.

Brighouse, T. and Woods, D. (1999) *How to Improve Your School*, London: Routledge.

Buchanan, D.A. and Huczynski, A.A. (1985) *Organizational Behaviour: An Introductory Text*, London: Prentice Hall.

Caldwell, B.J. and Spinks, J.M. (1998) *Beyond the Self-Managing School*, London: The Falmer Press.

Cava, R. (1990) *Dealing with Difficult People*, London: Judy Piatkus Publishers.

Chang, R.Y. and Curtin, M.J. (1994) *Succeeding as a Self-Managed Team*, London: Kogan Page.

Collins English Dictionary and Thesaurus (1993) Glasgow: HarperCollins.

Davies, J. (1985) 'Why are women not where the power is? An examination of the maintenance of power elites', *Management Education and Development* 16 (3), pp. 278–88.

References

Day, C., Harris, A., Hadfield, M., Tolley, H. and Beresford, J. (2000) *Leading Schools in Times of Change*, Buckingham: Open University Press.

DfEE (Department for Education and Employment) (1998) *Getting the Most from Your Data: Guidance Note*, London: DfEE Publications.

DfEE (2000a) *Performance Management in Schools: Performance Management Framework*, London: DfEE Publications.

DfEE (2000b) *Performance Management in Schools: Guidance Note*, London: DfEE Publications.

DfEE (2000c) *Performance Management in Schools: Model Performance Management Policy*, London: DfEE Publications.

DfEE (2000d) *Professional Development (Consultation Paper)*, London: DfEE Publications.

Drucker, P. (1970) *The Effective Executive*, London: Pan Books.

Egan, Sir J. (1998) Interview in the *Financial Times*, 26 January.

Eggleston, J. (2000) 'Whatever happened to the staffroom library?', *Times Educational Supplement*, April 28.

Emmerson, C. and Frayne, C. (2001) *Spending on Public Services: IFs Election Briefing Note*, No. 3, London: Institute of Fiscal Studies.

Evans, L. (1998) *Teacher Morale, Job Satisfaction and Motivation*, London: Paul Chapman.

Evans, R. (1996) *The Human Side of School Change*, San Francisco, CA: Jossey-Bass.

Everhard, K.B. and Morris, G. (1985) *Effective School Management*, London: Harper & Row.

Evetts, J. (1994) *Becoming a Secondary Headteacher*, London: Cassell.

Field, K., Holden, P. and Lawlor, H. (2000) *Effective Subject Leadership*, London: Routledge.

Fullan, M. and Hargreaves, A. (1992) *What's Worth Fighting For in Your School?* Buckingham: Open University Press.

Furnham, A. (2000) 'Thinking about intelligence', *The Psychologist* 13 (10), pp. 510–15.

Georgeiades, N.J. and Phillimore, L. (1975) 'The myth of the hero-innovator and alternative strategies for organizational change' in C. Kiernan and F.P. Woodford (eds), *Behaviour Modification with the Severely Retarded*, Oxford: Association of Scientific Publishers.

Gewirtz, S. (1998) 'Can all schools be successful: an exploration of the determinants of school "success"', *Oxford Review of Education* 14 (4), pp. 439–57.

Gewirtz, S., Ball, S.J. and Bowe, R. (1995) *Markets, Choice and Equity in Education*, Buckingham: Open University Press.

Glass, N.M. (1996) *Management Masterclass: A Practical Guide to the New Realities of Business*, London: Nicholas Brealey Publishing.

Goleman, D. (1998a) *Working with Emotional Intelligence*, London: Bloomsbury.

Goleman, D. (1998b) 'What makes a leader?', *Harvard Business Review*, November/December, pp. 93–201.

Goleman, D. (2000) 'Leadership that gets results', *Harvard Business Review*, March/April, pp. 78–90.

Gould, S.J. (1991) *Bully for Brontosaurus*, New York: Norton.

Grace, R. (1995) *School Leadership: Beyond Education Management*, London: The Falmer Press.

Gratton, L. (2000) *Living Strategy: Putting People at the Heart of Corporate Purpose*, London: Pearson Education.

Gronn, P. (1999) *The Making of Educational Leaders*, London: Cassell.

Hall, V. (1996) *Dancing on the Ceiling: A Study of Women Managers in Education*, London: Paul Chapman.

Handy, C. (1976) *Understanding Organizations*, Harmondsworth: Penguin.

Handy, C. (1996) Talk delivered at Schools Award Ceremony, London.

Handy, C. and Aitken, R. (1986) *Understanding Schools as Organizations*, London: Penguin Books.

Hargreaves, A. (1994) *Changing Teachers, Changing Times: Teachers' Work and Culture in the Postmodern Age*, London: Cassell.

Hargreaves, A. and Fullan, M. (1998) *What's Worth Fighting for in Education?*, Buckingham: Open University Press.

Heller, R. (2000) 'For a winning strategy only connect', *Observer*, 13 August.

Honey, P. (1980) *Solving People Problems*, London: McGraw-Hill.

Hutchings, M., Mentor, I., Ross, A., Thomson, D. with Bedford, D. (2000) *Teacher Supply and Retention in London 1998–99* (Report for the Teacher Training Agency), London: University of North London School of Education.

Jayne, E. (1989) 'Women as leaders of schools: The role of training', *Educational Management and Administration*, 17, pp. 109–14.

Johnson, M. (1999) *Failing School, Failing City: The Reality of Inner-City Education*, Charlbury: Jon Carpenter Publishing.

Jones, P. and Sparks, N. (1996) *Effective Heads of Department*, Stafford: Network Educational Press Ltd.

Katzenbach, J.R. and Smith, D.K. (1993) *The Wisdom of Teams*, Boston, MA: Harvard Business Press.

Kline, P. (1993) *Personality: The Psychometric View*, London: Routledge.

Lefcourt, H.M. (1991) 'Locus of control 413–499' in J.P. Robinson, P.R. Shaver and L.S. Wrightsman (eds) *Measures of Personality and Social Psychological Attitudes*, New York: Academic Press.

McCall, C. (1998) *School Self-Review Manual*, London: Financial Times/Pitman Publishing.

McCall, C. and Lawlor, H. (2000) *Leadership Examined*, London: The Stationery Office.

McClelland, D.C. (1987) *Human Motivation*, Cambridge: Cambridge University Press.

McClelland, D.C. and Burnham, D.H. (1976) 'Power is the great motivator', *Harvard Business Review*, March/April, pp. 100–10, 159–66.

McCormack, M.H. (1990) *The 110% Solution*, London: Chapmans.

McGregor, D. (1960) *The Human Side of the Enterprise*, New York: McGraw-Hill.

Martin, P., Harrison, D. and Dinitto, D. (1983) 'Advancement for women in hierarchical organizations: A multilevel analysis of problems and prospects', *The Journal of Applied Behavioural Science* 19 (1), pp. 19–33.

Mischel, W. (1999) *Introduction to Personality* (6th edn), New York: Harcourt Brace College Publishers.

Morley, L. and Rassool, N. (1999) *School Effectiveness: Fracturing the Discourse*, London: The Falmer Press.

Mumford, A. (1993) *How Managers Can Develop Managers*, London, Gower.

NAHT (National Association of Head Teachers) (2000) 'Headteacher Stress', survey reported in the *Independent*, 7 April.

Nolan, V. (1987) *The Innovator's Handbook*, London: Sphere Books Limited.

Norwich, B., Cooper, P. and Maras, P. (1999) 'Are children breaking down or is it the system?', *Independent*, 25 March.

O'Brien, P. (1993) *Taking the Macho out of Management*, London: Sheldon Press.

OECD (Organization for Economic Cooperation and Development) (2000) 'Britain near bottom of the class on pupil–teacher ratios', *Independent*, 17 May.

OFSTED (Office for Standards in Education) (1998a) Secondary Education 1993–7: *A Review of Secondary Schools in England*, London: OFSTED Publications Centre.

OFSTED (1998b) *School Evaluation Matters*, London: DfEE.

OFSTED (1999) *Handbook for Inspecting Secondary Schools*, London: The Stationery Office.

Owen, H. (2000) *Creating Top Flight Teams*, London: Kogan Page.

Pearce, B. (1998) *Reviewing as a Tool for Managers and Leaders*, London: Teacher Training Agency.

Peters, T.J. and Waterman, R.H. (1982) *In Search of Excellence: Lessons from America's Best Run Companies*, New York: Harper and Row.

Robbins, H. and Finley, M. (1997) *Why Change Doesn't Work*, London: Orion Business Books.

Rotter, J.B. (1966) 'Generalised expectancies for internal versus external control of reinforcement', *Psychological Monographs* 80 (609).

Sammons, P., Thomas, S. and Mortimore, P. (1997) *Forging Links*, London: Paul Chapman.

Schein, E.H. (1985) *Organisational Culture and Leadership*, San Francisco, CA: Jossey-Bass.

Schon, D. (1983) *The Reflective Practitioner*, London: Temple Smith.

School Teachers' Review Body (2000) 'Teacher hours continue to rise', *Times Educational Supplement*, 11 July.

Senge, P (1990) *The Fifth Discipline*, New York: Doubleday.

Starratt, R. (1995) *Leaders with Vision: The Quest for School Renewal*, Thousand Oaks, CA: Corwin Press.

Stress Teacherline (2000) 'Stress on the emotional landscape', *Times Educational Supplement*, 10 November, and *Independent*, 24 March.

Stoll, L. and Fink, D. (1996) *Changing Our Schools: Linking School Effectiveness and School Improvement*, Buckingham: Open University Press.

Stoll, L. and Mortimore, P. (1995) *School Effectiveness and School Improvement*, Viewpoint No. 2, London: Institute of Education, University of London.

Talbot, M. (2000) *Make Your Mission Statement Work: How to Identify and Promote the Values of your Organisation*, Oxford: How To Books.

Tate, N. (1999) 'Standards are up', *Independent*, 16 September.

TES (2000) News section, *Times Educational Supplement*, 7 April.

Thomas, G., Walker, D. and Webb, J. (1998) *The Making of the Inclusive School*, London: Routledge.

Tooley, J. (1997) 'Better choice than producer whim', *Times Educational Supplement*, 31 January.

Toynbee, P. (1998) 'The estate they're in', *Guardian*, 15 September.

TTA (1995) *Survey of Continuing Professional Development* (research conducted for the TTA by MORI), London: Teacher Training Agency.

TTA (1998) *Teaching as a Research-Based Profession*, London: Teacher Training Agency.

TTA (2000) *Career Entry Profile 2000: Notes on Guidance and Standards*, London: Teacher Training Agency.

Turner, D. (1998) *Liberating Leadership: A Manager's Guide to the New Leadership*, London: The Industrial Society.

References

Weiner, G. (1994) *Feminisms in Education: An Introduction*, London: Open University Press.

Weiss, A. (1989) *Managing for Peak Performance*, New York: Harper & Row.

West-Burnham, J. and O'Sullivan, F. (1998) *Leadership and Professional Development in Schools*, London: Financial Times/Pitman Publishing.

White, J. (1998) *Do Howard Gardner's Multiple Intelligences Add Up?*, London: Institute of Education, University of London.

Wilby, P. (1997) 'Let's choose catchment area, not market force', *Times Educational Supplement*, 17 January.

Willms, J.D. (1992) *Monitoring School Performance: A Guide for Educators*, London: The Falmer Press.

Woods, D. and Orlik, S. (1994) *School Review and Inspection*, London: Kogan Page.

Zohar, D. and Marshall, I.N. (2000) *SQ – Spiritual Intelligence: The Ultimate Intelligence*, London: Bloomsbury.

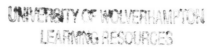

Index by Sylvia Potter